Discovering Life Skills

Teacher Resource Guide

Mc Graw Hill **Glencoe**

New York, New York   Columbus, Ohio   Chicago, Illinois   Peoria, Illinois   Woodland Hills, California

Contributor:

Linda Perrin, Yardley, Pennsylvania

Send all inquiries to:
Glencoe/McGraw-Hill
3008 W. Willow Knolls Drive
Peoria, IL 61614-1083

ISBN 0-07-846239-8

Printed in the United States of America

3 4 5 6 7 8 9 10   047   07 06 05 04

Table of Contents

Student Edition

◀ ***Discovering Life Skills*** is divided into four units and 25 chapters. Each chapter opener lists the objectives and key terms for that chapter. These key terms appear in boldface type on the chapter pages. An opening paragraph invites students to discover the topics contained in the chapter.

How to... features help students discover how to use their knowledge to apply what they've learned. These single-page topics can be pulled out as special projects or used as an integral part of the chapter. ▼

Explore... features encourage students to explore various topics through research, hands-on experiences, or group discussions. These single-page topics can be used as an integral part of the chapter or pulled out for separate study.

▶

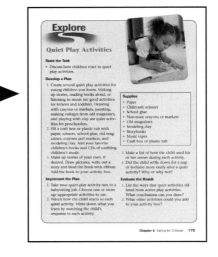

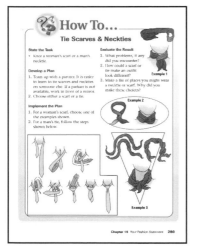

Internet Activities features direct students to use the Internet to find out more information about a topic and to share their findings. An "Internet Permissions Agreement" form can be found on page 14 of this *Teacher Resource Guide.*

▶

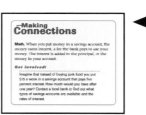

◀ ***Making Connections*** features link student learning with mathematics, social studies, science, language arts, and technology.

Discovering Life Skills

Student Edition (continued)

A Closer Look... features provide a focused look at a particular topic that relates to each chapter. These 25 two-page spreads are great for class discussions and can lead to further assignments.

Career Choices features introduce five careers that relate to the chapter content. These careers include choices within and outside of Family & Consumer Sciences.

Safety First features draw students' attention to matters of safety.

Check the Facts features provide interesting tidbits of information that students may want to research further.

Did You Know features give students more information on a topic of interest at the point that the topic interfaces with chapter content.

Chapter Review & Activities feature a chapter summary, vocabulary questions, review questions, and application activities. These single-pages will allow students to easily review what they have learned.

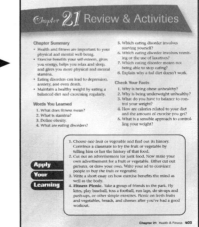

Just for Fun features offer students fun ideas to try outside of class.

Student Workbook

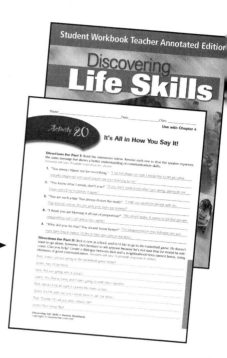

The *Student Workbook* provides over 130 activity worksheets that will reinforce chapter content. Students will be engaged by the variety of worksheets provided.

Answers are printed in color in the *Student Workbook Teacher Annotated Edition*. This teacher edition will help you grade worksheets quickly!

Project & Activity Cards

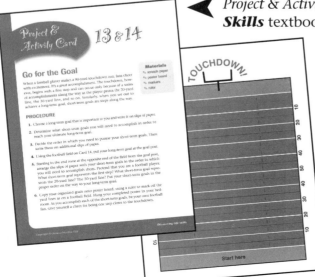

Project & Activity Cards complement the ***Discovering Life Skills*** textbook and give students opportunities to explore additional life skills topics. These laminated, 8½" × 11" cards contain 43 separate projects and activities. Students can work with the cards independently or in small groups. You will find a set of *Project & Activity Cards* in the *Student Motivation Kit* (see page 7). However, you may want to purchase additional sets for your classroom (refer to ISBN 0-07-846247-9).

Student Motivation Kit

This valuable collection of reproducible resources is packed full of student-focused materials! Each page can be used to supplement the textbook content. Many activities can also serve as expansion pieces for further study. Your students will thrive on the wide variety of interesting activities contained in this *Student Motivation Kit.* A short description of each item in the kit follows.

- ◆ **Project & Activity Cards** give students opportunities to explore additional life skills topics. These laminated, 8½" × 11" cards contain 43 separate projects and activities. Students can work with the cards independently or in small groups. Your students will have so much fun with these cards that you may want to have more than one set for your classroom! They can be purchased separately as ISBN 0-07-846247-9.

- ◆ **Foods Labs** contains reproducible activity sheets for use in the foods lab or at home. Students will enjoy trying out new techniques and recipes.

- ◆ **Sewing Labs** contains reproducible sewing projects to be used with the clothing and housing chapters in the textbook. Students can express their creativity as well as learn valuable life skills by completing these projects.

- ◆ **Career Investigations** contains reproducible activity sheets that ask students to investigate careers within and outside of Family & Consumer Sciences.

- ◆ **Reteaching Activities** contains reproducible worksheets that reinforce chapter content found in the textbook. Students often retain more when asked to learn the same information in different ways.

- ◆ **Enrichment Activities** contains reproducible activities that expand learning beyond the textbook. Some of these activities are projects and take longer than one class period. Students can enjoy these activities at school or at home.

Teacher Resource Guide

Teaching Discovering Life Skills offers suggestions for scope and sequence, aligning FCS modules, Internet permission, a program advisory committee, FCCLA, learning approaches, thinking skills, teaching special needs students, and assessment strategies.

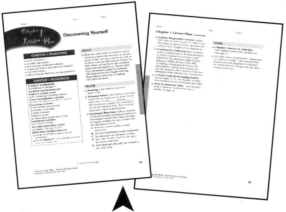

Lesson Plans provide a list of chapter objectives, chapter resources from the *Discovering Life Skills* program, and teaching suggestions to *Focus, Assess, Teach,* and *Close* each chapter of the student textbook.

Chapter Review & Activities
Answer Key provides a convenient list of answers to the questions that appear at the end of each textbook chapter.

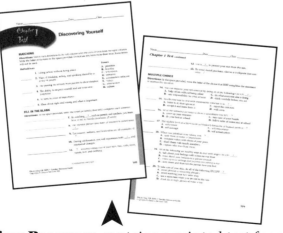

Testing Program Answer Key provides a convenient list of answers to each of the printed chapter tests found in the *Testing Program*.

Testing Program contains a printed test for each of the 25 chapters in the textbook. There are either 20 or 25 items on each chapter test. Each test contains three different types of test items.

Discovering Life Skills • Teacher Resource Guide
Copyright © Glencoe/McGraw-Hill

Additional Resources

Internet Disclaimer

The following Internet listings are a source of extended information related to our text. We have made every effort to recommend sites that are informative and accurate. However, these sites are not under the control of Glencoe/McGraw-Hill, and therefore Glencoe/McGraw-Hill makes no representation concerning the content of these sites. We strongly encourage teachers to preview Internet sites before students use them. Many sites contain links to other sites, and following such links may eventually lead to exposure to inappropriate material. Internet sites are sometimes "under construction" and may not always be available. Sites may also move or have been discontinued completely by the time you or your students attempt to access them.

MODULE SUPPLIERS

Applied Educational Systems, Inc.

www.aeseducation.com

Provides Life Center 21™ modules for Family & Consumer Sciences Education.

CHEC Systems, a division of DEPCO, Inc.

www.checsystems.com

Provides modules for Family & Consumer Sciences Education.

Hearlihy & Company

www.hearlihy.com

Provides modules for Family & Consumer Sciences Education.

Lab-Volt Systems, Inc.

www.labvolt.com

Provides Tech-Design® modules for Family & Consumer Sciences Education.

Paxton/Patterson

www.paxtonpatterson.com

Provides EduSystems™ modules for Family & Consumer Sciences Education.

Synergistic Systems

www.synergistic-systems.com

Provides modules for Family & Consumer Sciences Education.

ORGANIZATIONS

American Association of Family & Consumer Sciences (AAFCS)

www.aafcs.org

AAFCS is a national organization that represents Family & Consumer Sciences professionals. This site links resources to the 16 National Family & Consumer Sciences Teaching Standards.

Family, Career and Community Leaders of America (FCCLA)

www.fcclainc.org

FCCLA is a nonprofit national organization for secondary school students in Family & Consumer Sciences Education.

Find the column that best describes the length of your program. Then read down to find the suggested number of class periods for each chapter of the text. Use the far right column to adapt the suggestions to your own program.

Discovering Life Skills ©2004	6-Week Program	9-Week Program	18-Week Program	Your Program
Ch. 1: Discovering Yourself	2	3	4	
Ch. 2: Your Family	1	2	4	
Ch. 3: Your Friendships	1	2	4	
Ch. 4: Communicating With Others	1	1	3	
Ch. 5: Citizenship & Leadership	1	1	2	
Ch. 6: Managing Your Life	1	2	4	
Ch. 7: Exploring Careers	4	5	5	
Ch. 8: Employability Skills	1	1	3	
Ch. 9: Caring for Children	2	2	4	
Ch. 10: Babysitting Basics	1	1	3	
Ch. 11: Managing Your Money	1	2	3	
Ch. 12: Managing Your Resources	2	2	4	
Ch. 13: Your Living Space	1	2	4	
Ch. 14: Your Environment	1	1	3	
Ch. 15: Your Fashion Statement	1	1	2	
Ch. 16: Clothing Basics	1	2	4	
Ch. 17: Preparing to Sew	1	1	2	
Ch. 18: Sewing & Serging Basics	1	2	5	
Ch. 19: Expressing Creativity	0	1	4	
Ch. 20: Nutrition & Wellness	1	2	4	
Ch. 21: Health & Fitness	1	2	3	
Ch. 22: Working in the Kitchen	1	1	3	
Ch. 23: Preparing to Cook	1	2	5	
Ch. 24: Cooking Basics	1	3	5	
Ch. 25: Microwave Basics	1	1	3	
TOTALS:	30	45	90	

MODULE CROSSWALK

The Module Crosswalk provides a breakdown of modules that can be used with *Discovering Life Skills*. Below is a list of modules that are offered by five different companies. Use the numbers next to each module listed below when referring to the chart on page 13.

Applied Educational Systems, Inc. Modules

1. Personal Appearance and Environment
2. Personal Development and Self-Esteem
3. Personal and Social Responsibility
4. Family Roles and Relationships
5. Interpersonal Relationships
6. Goal Setting and Career Planning
7. Human Growth and Development
8. Child Care
9. Consumer Education and Practices
10. Resource Management
11. Food Production and Services
12. Housing, Interiors, and Furnishings
13. Textiles and Apparel
14. Fashion and Design
15. Nutrition and Wellness

CHEC Systems, a division of DEPCO, Inc. Modules

16. Lasting Impressions: Image/Appearance
17. Human Asset Imaging™
18. Academic Integration
19. Internet: The World Wide Web
20. Family Portrait: Dependent Care
21. Balancing Act: Introduction to Work & Family
22. Brave New World: Introduction to Family & Consumer Sciences Technology
23. Perfect Touch: Parenting Responsibilities
24. Car Fever: Purchasing Automobiles
25. Outer Limits: Electronic Shopping
26. Signs of the Times: Money and Credit
27. Coming Clean: Home Care
28. The Magic Touch: Smart House
29. True Colors: Color in Every Day Life
30. Safe and Sound: Home Security
31. For Earth's Sake: Environment/Recycling
32. New Twist: High-Tech Fibers
33. Eat and Run: Food for Working Families
34. Getting the Fat Out: Healthy Lifestyles

Lab-Volt Modules

35. Making the Most of Me: Maturity and Self-Discovery
36. Look Good, Feel Good: Health and Hygiene
37. Family Life: Different Kinds of Families
38. Manners Matter: Etiquette
39. We the People: Model Citizenship
40. Get a Job: Employment
41. Skills and Competencies At-a-Glance
42. Child's Play: Responsible Caretaking
43. Dollars and Sense: Money Management
44. Better Shop Around: Consumerism
45. Fixer Upper: Basic Home Maintenance
46. Houses of Style: Interior Design
47. Passion for Fashion: Fashion Design
48. Wash Away: Laundering
49. Sew E-Z: Sewing
50. Food for Thought: Healthy Eating
51. Snack Attack: Making Snacks
52. Savor the Flavor: Herbs and Spices
53. Wake-Up Call: Cooking Breakfast
54. How Sweet It Is: Making Desserts

Paxton/Patterson Modules

55. Your Inner Self
56. Standing Strong
57. The Global Family
58. Friends Forever
59. Know-How in the Workplace
60. Caregiving
61. Child Care
62. Global Child
63. Parenting
64. Banking Services
65. Comparative Buying
66. The Credit Cycle
67. Consumer Protection
68. Color by Design
69. Facility Maintenance
70. Architectural Design
71. Spatial Planning
72. Fashion Fundamentals
73. Fabric Innovations
74. Nutritional Facts
75. Science in the Kitchen
76. Biology in the Kitchen
77. Food Science
78. Math in the Kitchen

Synergistic Systems Modules

79. Practical Skills
80. Families (Web Design)
81. Careers
82. Life Skills (Power Point)
83. Early Childhood
84. Entrepreneurship: Child Care
85. Personal Finance
86. Confident Consumer
87. Interior Design
88. Digital Design
89. Fashion & Textiles
90. Basic Sewing
91. Sewing & Design
92. Breakfast Nutrition
93. Fitness & Health
94. Heart Fitness
95. Snack Nutrition
96. Baking & Measurement

Discovering Life Skills ©2004	Applied Educational Systems, Inc. Modules	CHEC Systems, a division of DEPCO, Inc. Modules	Lab-Volt Modules	Paxton/ Patterson Modules	Synergistic Systems Modules
Ch. 1: Discovering Yourself	1, 2, 3	16, 17, 18, 19	35, 36	55, 56	79
Ch. 2: Your Family	3, 4	19, 20, 21	37	57	79, 80
Ch. 3: Your Friendships	3, 5	19		58	79
Ch. 4: Communicating With Others		18, 19			79
Ch. 5: Citizenship & Leadership	3	18, 19	38, 39		79
Ch. 6: Managing Your Life	3, 6	19			79
Ch. 7: Exploring Careers	6	19, 22	40, 41		79, 81
Ch. 8: Employability Skills		18, 19	40, 41	59	79, 82
Ch. 9: Caring for Children	7	19, 20, 23	42	60, 61, 62, 63	79, 83, 84
Ch. 10: Babysitting Basics	8	19, 20	42	60, 61	79, 83, 84
Ch. 11: Managing Your Money		18, 19, 24, 25, 26	43	64	79, 85
Ch. 12: Managing Your Resources	3, 9, 10, 11	18, 19, 24, 25	44	65, 66, 67	79, 86
Ch. 13: Your Living Space	12	18, 19, 27, 28, 29	45, 46	68, 69, 70, 71	79, 87, 88
Ch. 14: Your Environment	3	18, 19, 30, 31			79
Ch. 15: Your Fashion Statement	13, 14	18, 19, 29	47	72	79, 89
Ch. 16: Clothing Basics	13, 14	18, 19, 32	48	68, 73	79, 89
Ch. 17: Preparing to Sew		18, 19			79, 90
Ch. 18: Sewing & Serging Basics		19	49		79, 90, 91
Ch. 19: Expressing Creativity		19, 21, 29	47	73	79, 91
Ch. 20: Nutrition & Wellness	15	19, 33	50	74	79, 92
Ch. 21: Health & Fitness	15	19, 34			79, 93, 94
Ch. 22: Working in the Kitchen		19		75, 76, 77	79
Ch. 23: Preparing to Cook	15	18, 19	38, 51	78	79, 95, 96
Ch. 24: Cooking Basics	11	19, 33	52, 53, 54		79
Ch. 25: Microwave Basics		18, 19, 33	51		79, 92, 95

INTERNET PERMISSION AGREEMENT SAMPLE

This school is fortunate to have been equipped with access to the Internet. Our system has been established to help students learn and to help them develop their computer skills. It is our school's intention to use computers and the Internet responsibly.

BELOW IS A LIST OF RULES WE ABIDE BY. *ANY VIOLATION OF THESE RULES WILL BE MET WITH ZERO TOLERANCE.*

1. No personal contact information will be posted or shared on the Internet.

2. Students will report any inappropriate messages to their teacher.

3. Students will not engage in any illegal act, including plagiarizing content from the Internet.

4. Students will not use obscene language, engage in personal or discriminatory attacks, or post false or misleading information.

5. Students will not attempt to gain unauthorized access or disrupt any computer system by willfully destroying data or spreading viruses.

By signing below, I fully understand and agree with the contents of this Internet Permission Agreement. If I violate any rules, I understand my Internet and computer privileges will be revoked.

Signed by:

Student: _____ Date: _____

Teacher: _____ Date: _____

Parent or Guardian: _____ Date: _____

PROGRAM ADVISORY COMMITTEE

The use of a program advisory committee can be an effective means of keeping the community informed, keeping curriculum up-to-date, and selling the school board on the importance of Family and Consumer Sciences Courses.

The program advisory committee can help:
- ◆ Establish program goals.
- ◆ Give advice concerning curriculum.
- ◆ Create good rapport between area businesses and the school's Family and Consumer Sciences program.
- ◆ Assist with program evaluation.

To organize an advisory committee:
1. Check with your school board for policies regarding advisory committees.
2. Secure the names of people who are involved in various aspects of Family and Consumer Sciences Education.
3. Write each potential advisory committee member a letter asking for his or her service.
4. When the replies are received, send another letter thanking them for their willingness to serve and give a time and location for the first meeting.

It is best to ask advisory committee members to serve for a minimum of one year. That way, those members whose attendance is lacking may be dropped after one year. Remember to send a letter thanking them for their service. Then secure someone else to take his or her place. Those members who have been active may continue by mutual agreement. Committee membership should be rotated so that you are never working with a totally "new" committee.

FCCLA

Family, Career and Community Leaders of America, Inc. (FCCLA) is a nonprofit national student organization for young men and women enrolled in Family & Consumers Sciences courses. Involvement in FCCLA offers members the opportunity to expand their leadership potential, explore careers, and develop skills for life. Through FCCLA, students can participate in a number of programs and competitions to strengthen their skills and leadership abilities.

Career Connection. Through individual, cooperative, and competitive events, members discover their strengths, target career goals, and initiate a plan for living their chosen way of life. The activity areas offered in the *Career Connection* program include:
- ◆ Plug In to Careers.
- ◆ Sign On to the Career Connection.
- ◆ Program Career Steps.
- ◆ Link Up to Jobs.
- ◆ Access Skills for Career Success.
- ◆ Integrate Work and Life.

STAR Events. These competitive events recognize FCCLA members for proficiency and achievement in chapter and individual projects, leadership skills, and occupational preparation. Depending upon specific event rules and procedures, projects may be carried out by individuals or teams. National *STAR Event* participants are selected by state-established procedures before moving on to nationals. Some events include:
- ◆ Illustrated Talk.
- ◆ Job Interview.
- ◆ Entrepreneurship.

APPROACHES TO LEARNING

Learners have preferences for how they receive and interact with new information. Many approaches match learning experiences to learning preferences, or learning styles.

Most experts agree that we all have personality traits that affect how we perceive, interact with, and respond to learning situations. Opinions vary as to how to use learning preferences. Some think students should be grouped according to learning preferences. Others think this is unnecessary and may limit students.

Using a preferred style is motivating; however, using only one style is like exercising the one muscle you have that is already strong. Continual variety helps students become flexible learners. Using a variety of methods and media will balance out the styles of a wide variety of learners. Providing choices and multiple approaches in the learning environment is compatible with the brain's needs.

Brain-Based Learning. Many approaches to learning are based on brain-based learning. The brain is constantly evolving in response to stimulation. It thrives with exposure to a variety of experiences. Ideal conditions for stimulating the brain in learning environments include:

- A variety of learning experiences
- Learner choice
- A balance of novelty and predictability
- Adequate time for learning
- Moderate to high challenge level
- Encouragement
- Support of fellow students
- Low or no threat
- Frequent feedback
- Preparation for final performance

Learning Modalities. A common model for learning styles refers to the sensory modes that learners prefer when receiving information. The main types are visual (seeing), auditory (hearing), and kinesthetic (feeling). Visual learners prefer seeing, examining, and reading about things. Auditory learners think in sounds and prefer information that is presented orally. Kinesthetic learners prefer to manipulate objects and materials.

Consideration of these categories may affect the type of media you choose to present material. For example, many students are not strong in the auditory mode, which makes lectures an extra challenge for them. Other factors must also be considered when deciding which type of media to use for presenting materials. One is the learning goal. For example, the best way to demonstrate sounds is to use sound, whether or not the learners prefer auditory input.

In addition, younger learners or learners less experienced with a certain topic may benefit from more concrete, kinesthetic types of input as opposed to abstract input. As learners mature and gain more experience, they will develop their natural styles. Those that are not naturally kinesthetic will depend less on that style. They can more readily learn from abstract materials, which provide more detail.

Multiple Intelligences. Howard Gardner has identified nine types of intelligence. As with other models, students may vary widely in their strengths and weaknesses. Many students are not strong in the two categories often used most in school: linguistic and logical/mathematical. The chart on page 17 provides a variety of strategies for each of the intelligences.

MULTIPLE INTELLIGENCES

TYPE OF INTELLIGENCE	LEARNS BY...	IS GOOD AT...
Linguistic Intelligence is related to words and language, written and spoken.	◆ saying ◆ hearing ◆ seeing words	memorizing names, dates, places, and trivia; spelling; using descriptive language; and creating imaginary worlds
Logical/Mathematical Intelligence deals with inductive and deductive thinking and reasoning, numbers, and abstractions.	◆ categorizing ◆ classifying ◆ working with patterns and relationships	math, reasoning, logic, problem solving, computing numbers, moving from concrete to abstract, thinking conceptually
Spatial Intelligence relies on the sense of sight and being able to visualize an object, including the ability to create mental images.	◆ visualizing ◆ dreaming ◆ using the mind's eye ◆ working with colors and pictures	understanding the use of space and how to get around in it, thinking in three-dimensional terms, and imagining things in clear visual images
Bodily/Kinesthetic Intelligence is related to physical movement and the brain's motor cortex, which controls bodily movements.	◆ touching ◆ moving ◆ interacting with space ◆ processing knowledge through bodily sensations	physical activities such as sports, dancing, acting, and crafts
Musical/Rhythmic Intelligence is based on recognition of tonal patterns, including various environmental sounds, and on a sensitivity to rhythm and beats.	◆ rhythm ◆ melody ◆ music	remembering melodies; keeping time; mimicking beat and rhythm; noticing pitches, rhythms, and background and environmental sounds
Interpersonal Intelligence operates primarily through person-to-person relationships and communication.	◆ sharing ◆ comparing ◆ relating ◆ cooperating ◆ interviewing	understanding people and their feelings, leading others, organizing, communicating, manipulating, mediating conflicts
Intrapersonal Intelligence is related to inner states of being, self-reflection, metacognition, and awareness of spiritual realities.	◆ working alone ◆ doing individualized projects ◆ engaging in self-paced instruction	understanding self, focusing on feelings/dreams, following instincts, pursuing interests, and being original
Naturalistic Intelligence has to do with observing, understanding, and organizing patterns in the natural environment.	◆ visualizing ◆ hands-on activities ◆ relating to the natural world	measuring, charting, mapping, observing plants and animals, keeping journals, collecting, classifying, participating in outdoor activities

BUILDING THINKING SKILLS

Levels of Thinking. All learning requires thinking. Bloom's "Taxonomy of the Cognitive Domain" is a widely recognized model for levels of thinking.

Each of Bloom's cognitive categories includes a variety of thinking skills and the kind of behavior students are to perform as the objectives or goals of specific learning tasks.

◆ Students at any ability level can experience thinking at each level of the taxonomy.
◆ The levels build, one on the other. Students cannot be expected to operate at higher-level thinking without the necessary foundations.
◆ The level of complexity (from knowledge to evaluation) is not equal to the level of difficulty.

Level	Behavior		Questions & Activities
Knowledge	define recognize recall	identify label list	To prompt the identification and recall of information: ◆ Who, what, when, where, and how … ? ◆ Label the parts of … ?
Comprehension	translate interpret explain	describe summarize rewrite	To prompt the organization and selection of facts and ideas: ◆ Retell in your own words … ? ◆ What is the main idea of … ?
Application	apply solve experiment	show predict	To encourage the use of facts, rules, and principles: ◆ How is … an example of … ? ◆ How is … related to … ?
Analysis	relate classify group distinguish	organize categorize compare connect	To separate a whole into components parts: ◆ What are the parts or features of … ? ◆ Classify … according to … ? ◆ How does … compare/contrast with … ?
Synthesis	produce propose design plan combine	formulate compose hypothesize construct infer	To prompt the combination of ideas to form a new whole: ◆ What would you predict/infer from … ? ◆ What might happen if you combined … ?
Evaluation	appraise judge	criticize decide	To prompt the development of opinions, judgments, or decisions: ◆ What do you think about … ? ◆ Establish priorities for … ?

Critical Thinking. Critical thinking can be defined as the process of reasonably or logically deciding what to do or believe. Students need to:
◆ Understand her or his own and others' meaning and views
◆ Look for relationships, causes, inferences, theories, and patterns
◆ Look for alternatives
◆ Generate his or her own questions and activities
◆ Make judgments, choices, or decisions based on available information

Problem Solving. Student success in problem solving must be determined on an individual basis, not by comparison with the work of other students. Here are suggestions for directing problem-solving experiences.
◆ Encourage students to approach problems analytically.
◆ When appropriate, encourage students to work in small groups to solve problems.
◆ Dialogue among peers to discuss, explain, debate, or solve problems increases thinking and learning.

Discovering Life Skills • Teacher Resource Guide
Copyright © Glencoe/McGraw-Hill

Americans with Disabilities Act (ADA)

The Americans with Disabilities Act (ADA) defines individuals with disabilities as having a physical or mental impairment that substantially limits one or more major life activities. Major life activities are those that an average person can perform with little or no difficulty such as walking, breathing, seeing, hearing, speaking, learning, and working. Educational services must be designed to meet individual needs, and students with disabilities must be educated with nondisabled students.

Individuals with Disabilities Act (IDEA)

The Individuals with Disabilities Education Act (IDEA) provides for people with difficulties related to learning. The IDEA strengthens expectations and accountability for students with disabilities and bridges the gap that sometimes occurs between what students with disabilities learn and what is required in a regular classroom.

Under IDEA, a student with a disability may have a physical, emotional, learning, or behavioral problem that is educationally related and requires special education and related services. The categories include autism, deaf-blindness, developmental delay, emotional/behavioral disorder, hearing impairment, mental impairment, multiple impairments, orthopedic impairment, other health impairment, specific learning disability, speech and/or language impairment, traumatic brain injury, and visual impairment (including blindness).

Individualized Education Program (IEP)

The IDEA requires that each public school student who receives special education and related services for a disability must have an Individualized Education Program (IEP). The IEP creates an opportunity for teachers, parents, school administrators, related services personnel, and students (when appropriate) to work together to improve educational results for students with disabilities. The IEP guides the delivery of special education supports and services for the student with a disability.

Here are the steps taken to establish an IEP:

1. **Student is identified.** A school professional or parent may ask for an evaluation. Parents must approve the evaluation.
2. **Student is evaluated.** The evaluation must assess the student in all areas related to the student's suspected disability.
3. **Eligibility is decided.** A group of qualified professionals and the parents look at the student's evaluation results. Together, they decide if the student is a "child with a disability," as defined by IDEA. Parents may ask for a hearing to challenge the eligibility decision.
4. **Student is found eligible for services.** If the student is found to be a "child with a disability," as defined by IDEA, he or she is eligible for related services. The IEP team meets to write an IEP for the student.
5. **Services are provided.** Parents are given a copy of the IEP. Each of the student's teachers and service providers has access to the IEP, listing the accommodations, modifications, and supports that must be provided to the student.
6. **Progress is measured and reported.** The student's progress toward the annual goals is measured, and reported to the parents.
7. **IEP is reviewed.** The student's IEP is reviewed by the IEP team at least once a year, or more often if the parents or school ask for a review.
8. **Student is reevaluated.** At least every three years the student must be reevaluated. The purpose of the evaluation is to find out if the student continues to be a "child with a disability," as defined by IDEA, and what the student's educational needs are. The student may be reevaluated more often if conditions warrant, or if the student's parent or teacher asks for a new evaluation.

MEETING SPECIAL NEEDS

SPECIAL NEED	TIPS FOR INSTRUCTION
Learning Disabled. These students have a problem in one or more areas, such as academic learning, language, perceptions, social-emotional adjustment, memory, or ability to pay attention.	◆ Break down tasks and provide step-by-step prompts. ◆ Provide assistance and direction; clearly define rules, assignments, and duties. ◆ Allow for interaction during class time; use peer helpers. ◆ Practice skills frequently. ◆ Distribute outlines of material presented in class. ◆ Maintain student interest with games.
Limited English Proficiency (LEP). Some students speak English as a second language. Customs and behavior of people in the majority culture may be confusing for some of these students. Cultural values may inhibit some students from full participation in the classroom.	◆ Keep in mind that students' ability to speak English does not reflect their academic ability. ◆ Try to incorporate students' cultural experiences into your instruction. ◆ Include information about different cultures in the curriculum to help build students' self-image. ◆ Avoid cultural stereotypes.
Physically Challenged. Students who are physically disabled fall into two categories—those with orthopedic impairments (use of one or more limbs; severely restricted) and those with other health impairments.	◆ Help other students and adults understand physically disabled students. ◆ Learn about special devices or procedures and if any special safety precautions are needed. ◆ Allow students to participate in all activities. ◆ With the student, determine when you should offer aid, including field trips, special events, and projects.
Visually Impaired. These students have partial or total loss of sight. Individuals with visual impairments are not significantly different from their sighted peers in ability range or personality. However, blindness may affect cognitive, motor, and social development.	◆ Modify assignments as needed to help students become more independent. ◆ Tape lectures and reading assignments for the visually impaired. ◆ Encourage students to use their sense of touch; provide tactile models whenever possible. ◆ Verbally describe people and events as they occur in the classroom.
Hearing Impaired. These students who are hearing impaired have partial or total loss of hearing. Individuals with hearing impairments are not significantly different from their peers in ability range or personality. However, the chronic condition of deafness may affect cognitive, motor, social, and speech development.	◆ Provide favorable seating arrangements so hearing-impaired students can see speakers and read their lips (or interpreters can assist). ◆ Write out all instructions on paper or on the board; overhead projectors enable you to maintain eye contact while writing. ◆ Avoid standing with your back to the window or light source.
Gifted. Although no formal definition exists, these students can be described as having above average ability, task commitment, and creativity. They rank in the top five percent of their classes. They usually finish work more quickly than other students, and are capable of divergent thinking.	◆ Emphasize concepts, theories, relationships, ideas, and generalizations. ◆ Let students express themselves in a variety of ways including drawing, or acting. ◆ Allow students to work on independent projects. ◆ Make arrangements for students to take selected subjects early.
Behaviorally Disordered. Students with behavior disorders deviate from standards or expectations of behavior and impair the functioning of others and themselves. These students may also be gifted or learning disabled.	◆ Talk with students about their strengths and weaknesses, and clearly outline objectives and tell how you will help them obtain their goals. ◆ Structure schedules, rules, room arrangement, and safety for a conducive learning environment. ◆ Model appropriate behavior for students and reinforce proper behavior. ◆ Adjust group requirements for individual needs.

ASSESSMENT STRATEGIES

STRATEGIES	ADVANTAGES	DISADVANTAGES
Objective Measures ◆ Multiple choice ◆ Matching ◆ Item sets ◆ True/false	◆ Reliable, easy to validate ◆ Objective, if designed effectively ◆ Low cost, efficient ◆ Automated administration ◆ Lends to equating	◆ Measures cognitive knowledge effectively ◆ Limited on other measures ◆ Not a good measure of overall performance
Written Measures ◆ Essays ◆ Restricted response ◆ Written simulations ◆ Case analysis ◆ Problem-solving exercises	◆ Face validity (real life) ◆ In-depth assessment ◆ Measures writing skills and higher level skills ◆ Reasonable developmental costs and time	◆ Subjective scoring ◆ Time consuming and expensive to score ◆ Limited breadth ◆ Difficult to equate ◆ Moderate reliability
Oral Measures ◆ Oral examinations ◆ Interviews	◆ Measures communications and interpersonal skills ◆ In-depth assessment with varied stimulus materials ◆ Learner involvement	◆ Costly and time consuming ◆ Limited reliability ◆ Narrow sample of content ◆ Scoring difficult, need multiple raters
Simulated Activities ◆ Role play ◆ Computer simulations	◆ Moderate reliability ◆ Performance-based measure	◆ Costly and time consuming ◆ Difficult to score, administer, and develop
Portfolio and Product Analysis ◆ Work samples ◆ Projects ◆ Work diaries and logs ◆ Achievement records	◆ Provides information not normally available ◆ Learner involvement ◆ Face validity (real life) ◆ Easy to collect information	◆ Costly to administer ◆ Labor and paper intensive ◆ Difficult to validate or equate ◆ Biased toward best samples or outstanding qualities
Performance Measures ◆ Demonstrations ◆ Presentations ◆ Performances ◆ Rubrics ◆ Observation	◆ Job-related ◆ Relatively easy to administer ◆ In-depth assessment ◆ Face validity (real life)	◆ Rater training required ◆ Hard to equate ◆ Subjective scoring ◆ Time consuming if breadth is needed
Performance Records ◆ References ◆ Performance rating forms ◆ Parental rating	◆ Efficient ◆ Low cost ◆ Easy to administer	◆ Low reliability ◆ Subjective ◆ Hard to equate ◆ Rater judgment
Self-evaluation ◆ Rubrics ◆ Checklists	◆ Learner involvement and empowerment ◆ Learner responsibility ◆ Measures dimensions not available otherwise	◆ May be biased or unrealistic

Lesson Plans

Contents

Discovering Yourself

CHAPTER 1 OBJECTIVES

Students will discover...

◆ a positive self-concept.
◆ how to accept constructive criticism.
◆ helpful ways to deal with your emotions.
◆ your value system.
◆ physical changes that occur during adolescence.

CHAPTER 1 RESOURCES

STUDENT WORKBOOK
❑ Worksheet #1 through #7

STUDENT MOTIVATION KIT
Project & Activity Cards
❑ #3: Comparing Grooming Products
Career Investigation Activities
❑ Career Activity #1, 4, 5, 70, 71, 72 & 73
Reteaching Activities
❑ Put Your Best Foot Forward
❑ Everyday Living Skills
❑ Terms of Success
❑ Steps to Success
❑ Actions Speak Louder Than Words
Enrichment Activities
❑ Crossing the Bridge

TEACHER RESOURCE GUIDE
❑ Chapter 1 Test, pp. 103-104

EFFECTIVE INSTRUCTION CD
❑ Use the Word® file to tailor your own Lesson Plan.
❑ Use the **ExamView**® Test Generator to create your own chapter test.

FOCUS

❑ Hand out index cards on which you have written an emotional state such as *nervous, proud, excited, sad, angry,* and so on. Call on students to act out the emotion written on their index card and have class members guess what the emotion is. Discuss other ways the emotion might be expressed. Tell students that this chapter will help them learn positive ways of dealing with their emotions.

TEACH

❑ **Reading.** Have students read text pages 21-40.

❑ **Personal Values.** Ask students to identify values that are important to them. On the board write "I value _____ because _____." Ask students to complete the sentence in at least five different ways. Have students share their values in small groups.

❑ **Emotional Reactions.** Call on students to describe possible emotional reactions to the scenarios listed below. Then ask them to suggest constructive ways to deal with the emotions involved.
  A. Someone spreads unkind rumors about you.
  B. You can't understand a math assignment.
  C. You must give an oral report in class.
  D. Your older brother won't let you go to the movies with him.
  E. Your friend gets the part you wanted in the school play.

(Continued on next page)

Chapter 1 Lesson Plan continued

❏ **Explore Responsible Choices.** Assign the *Explore* activity on page 27. Hold a class discussion on self-destructive behavior after students have completed the assignment.

❏ **Constructive Criticism.** Have students work in small groups to develop situations in which constructive criticism is used effectively. The situations might include helping a sibling develop a new skill, or helping a friend practice for an oral presentation. Call on each group to act out one situation. Have the rest of the class determine if the criticism was constructive.

❏ **A Closer Look at Grooming Habits.** Discuss pages 34-35. Ask students to share their reactions to the information provided.

❏ **How to Manicure Nails.** Have students work in pairs to complete the *How To* activity on page 39.

ASSESS

❏ Use the reproducible Chapter 1 Test on page 103 of this *Teacher Resource Guide,* or construct your own test using the **Exam** *View* ® Test Generator found on the *Effective Instruction CD-ROM.*

CLOSE

❏ **Chapter 1 Review & Activities.** Have students answer the questions on text page 41.

❏ As a class, create a display titled "Adolescence Is a Time of Change." Have students find illustrations from magazines to illustrate the many different changes that take place during adolescence.

Your Family

CHAPTER 2 OBJECTIVES

Students will discover…

◆ the importance of families.
◆ several types of family structures.
◆ how to strengthen family relationships.
◆ ways to get along with family members.
◆ the changes that occur throughout the family life cycle.
◆ ways to adjust to changes that affect families.

CHAPTER 2 RESOURCES

STUDENT WORKBOOK
❏ Worksheet #8 through #12

STUDENT MOTIVATION KIT
Project & Activity Cards
❏ #4: Holiday Banners
❏ #5: Papier-Mâché Ornaments

Career Investigation Activities
❏ Career Activity #20, 21, 22 & 23

Reteaching Activities
❏ Establishing Family Traditions
❏ Getting Along With Family Members

Enrichment Activities
❏ Family Cookbook
❏ Place Mat Pizzazz

TEACHER RESOURCE GUIDE
❏ Chapter 2 Test, pp. 105-106

EFFECTIVE INSTRUCTION CD
❏ Use the Word® file to tailor your own Lesson Plan.
❏ Use the **ExamView**® Test Generator to create your own chapter test.

FOCUS

❏ Ask students to think of different ways to complete the sentence " A family is _____." Point out that there are many definitions of family because there are so many types of families. Tell students that this chapter will help them understand family relationships and responsibilities.

TEACH

❏ **Reading.** Have students read text pages 43-58.

❏ **Family Ties.** Make a classroom collage titled "Strengthen Family Ties." Hand out pieces of construction paper cut in the shape of neckties. Ask students to write a technique for strengthening family bonds on their ties. Possible ideas include going to the movies or on a picnic together.

❏ **Paying Compliments.** Ask students to write the name of a sibling or another family member at the top of a piece of paper. Then have them fold the paper in half lengthwise. In the left column have them list five characteristics they admire about the person. In the right column have them write a compliment to give the person based on each of the five characteristics. Encourage students to follow through and give the compliments to their family members.

(Continued on next page)

Chapter 2 Lesson Plan continued

❏ **Communication.** Brainstorm with the class creative ways of staying in touch with family members who live far away. Encourage students to explore different ways of sending photos as well as different ways of sending written, spoken, and printed messages.

❏ **Explore Family Responsibilities.** Assign the *Explore* activity on page 50. Invite volunteers to bring their schedules to class and explain how their plan is working.

❏ **Planning for Change.** Ask students to predict the kinds of changes they expect when they go to high school. You might invite several high school students to describe the changes they experienced and give suggestions for coping with changes.

❏ **A Closer Look at Relaxing Family Activities.** Discuss pages 52-53. Ask students to share their reactions to the information provided.

❏ **How to Plan a Family Evening at Home.** Ask students to complete the *How To* activity on page 57. Invite volunteers to describe how the evening turned out.

ASSESS

❏ Use the reproducible Chapter 2 Test on page 105 of this *Teacher Resource Guide,* or construct your own test using the **Exam***View*® Test Generator found on the *Effective Instruction CD-ROM.*

CLOSE

❏ **Chapter 2 Review & Activities.** Have students answer the questions on text page 59.

❏ Have students describe a scenario of a major change in a family and the steps the family took to cope.

Name_____ Date_____ Class _____

Your Friendships

CHAPTER 3 OBJECTIVES

Students will discover…

◆ the qualities of friendship.
◆ why friendships may change.
◆ the positive and negative influences of peer pressure.
◆ ways to handle peer pressure.
◆ how to be assertive.

CHAPTER 3 RESOURCES

STUDENT WORKBOOK
❏ Worksheet #13 through #17

STUDENT MOTIVATION KIT
Project & Activity Cards
❏ #6: Painted Mugs
❏ #7-8: Friendship Bracelets
Career Investigation Activities
❏ Career Activity #24, 25, 26 & 27
Reteaching Activities
❏ Handling Peer Pressure
❏ Harmful Substances
Enrichment Activities
❏ Decorative Gift Bags
❏ Decorative Picture Frames
❏ Listening Carefully

TEACHER RESOURCE GUIDE
❏ Chapter 3 Test, pp. 107-108

EFFECTIVE INSTRUCTION CD
❏ Use the Word® file to tailor your own Lesson Plan.
❏ Use the **ExamView**® Test Generator to create your own chapter test.

FOCUS

❏ Ask students to think of different ways to complete the sentence " A true friend is someone who _____." Point out that true friends are encouraging and supportive, and do not try to pressure others into taking risks. Tell students that this chapter will help them understand friendship, and the difference between positive and negative peer pressure.

TEACH

❏ **Reading.** Have students read text pages 61-76.
❏ **Making New Friends.** Write on the board an example of an "icebreaker"— a way of starting a conversation—such as "Did you go to the game last night?" Point out that effective icebreakers give the other person an opportunity to answer with more than just a yes or a no. Have students write at least three questions that make good icebreakers. Ask them to share their ideas with the entire class.
❏ **Explore Places to Meet New Friends.** Assign the *Explore* activity on page 64. Arrange to compile a master list of students' findings and post it in the classroom.
❏ **Keeping Friends.** On the board write the following reasons why teens have friends: similar interests, similar values, personal qualities, same school, same neighborhood. Have students discuss which category is most likely to lead to a lasting friendship, and why.

(Continued on next page)

Chapter 3 Lesson Plan continued

❏ **Assertiveness.** Write the following assertiveness tips on the board:
- Be firm.
- Stand up for yourself.
- Speak with confidence.
- Don't give in.

Have pairs of students role play the following scenarios, using assertive responses:

A. A friend wants you to skip school and go to the mall.

B. A friend forgot to do her homework and asks to copy yours.

C. A friend encourages you to smoke.

D. A friend urges you to take something from a store without paying for it.

❏ **A Closer Look at Saying "NO."** Discuss pages 72-73. Ask students to share their reactions to the information provided.

Special Note: Some adolescent psychologists argue that just saying "NO" is not a good approach because of the personal fable theory, where children think nothing bad will ever happen to them.

❏ **How to Walk Away.** Have students work in small groups to complete the *How To* activity on page 75.

ASSESS

❏ Use the reproducible Chapter 3 Test on page 107 of this *Teacher Resource Guide*, or construct your own test using the **Exam***View*® Test Generator found on the *Effective Instruction CD-ROM*.

CLOSE

❏ **Chapter 3 Review & Activities.** Have students answer the questions on text page 77.

❏ Discuss with students how an understanding of personal values and a strong self-concept can help teens handle peer pressure responsibly.

Communicating With Others

CHAPTER 4 OBJECTIVES

Students will discover...
- ◆ how to better communicate with others.
- ◆ the importance of being an effective listener.
- ◆ the importance of asking questions.
- ◆ reasons why conflicts occur.
- ◆ how to resolve conflicts.

CHAPTER 4 RESOURCES

STUDENT WORKBOOK
❑ Worksheet #18 through #24

STUDENT MOTIVATION KIT
Project & Activity Cards
❑ # 9: Causes of Conflict
❑ #10: Listening Skills

Career Investigation Activities
❑ Career Activity #29, 30, 31, 32 & 33

Reteaching Activities
❑ Conflict Resolution
❑ Nonverbal Communication

Enrichment Activities
❑ Making Decisions
❑ Resolving Conflicts

TEACHER RESOURCE GUIDE
❑ Chapter 4 Test, pp. 109-110

EFFECTIVE INSTRUCTION CD
❑ Use the Word® file to tailor your own Lesson Plan.
❑ Use the **ExamView**® Test Generator to create your own chapter test.

FOCUS

❑ Ask students to describe different ways of communicating an emotion such as happiness or sadness. Stress that there are many different ways to communicate, but for a message to be effective it must not only be sent but must also be understood. Tell students that in this chapter they will learn how to communicate effectively.

TEACH

❑ **Reading.** Have students read text pages 79-92.

❑ **Communication Collage.** Organize the class into small groups. Have students look through magazines and cut out pictures that illustrate verbal and nonverbal communication. Ask the groups to combine the pictures into one collage titled "What Is Communication?" Display the collage in the classroom.

❑ **Long-distance Communication.** Discuss with students the advantages and disadvantages of long-distance communication methods such as the telephone and e-mail. Emphasize the importance of speaking and writing clearly when there are no nonverbal clues to aid communication. Ask why misunderstandings are more likely with these forms of communication than with face-to-face communication.

(Continued on next page)

Chapter 4 Lesson Plan continued

❏ **The Art of Conversation.** Discuss with students what conversation is, and what makes it interesting. Ask them to analyze conversations they have enjoyed in the past, and explain what made them enjoyable. Use their responses to create a list of the elements of a good conversation. Then ask, "Is conversation a skill or an art?"

❏ **A Closer Look at Body Language.** Discuss pages 82-83. Ask students to share their reactions to the information provided.

❏ **Explore Creating a School Newsletter.** Assign the *Explore* activity on page 85. Encourage students to brainstorm ideas and share responsibilities.

❏ **Conflict Resolution.** Ask volunteers to describe a recent conflict. Have them describe the cause of the conflict, how the conflict could have been prevented, and how it was resolved. Have students suggest alternative resolutions to the conflict.

❏ **How to Conduct Peer Mediation.** Have students work in groups of three to complete the *How To* activity on page 91.

ASSESS

❏ Use the reproducible Chapter 4 Test on page 109 of this *Teacher Resource Guide*, or construct your own test using the **Exam***View*® Test Generator found on the *Effective Instruction CD-ROM*.

CLOSE

❏ **Chapter 4 Review & Activities.** Have students answer the questions on text page 93.

❏ Have students answer the following question: Why are both good speaking skills and good listening skills necessary for effective communication?

Citizenship & Leadership

CHAPTER 5 OBJECTIVES

Students will discover...
- ◆ ways to be a good citizen.
- ◆ ways to build and demonstrate leadership skills.
- ◆ how team members work together to achieve goals.

CHAPTER 5 RESOURCES

STUDENT WORKBOOK
- ❏ Worksheet #25 through #29

STUDENT MOTIVATION KIT
Project & Activity Cards
- ❏ #11: Book Covers
- ❏ #12: Canned Food Drive

Career Investigation Activities
- ❏ Career Activity #16, 24, 25, 27 & 28

Reteaching Activities
- ❏ Using Good Manners

Enrichment Activities
- ❏ Greeting Cards

TEACHER RESOURCE GUIDE
- ❏ Chapter 5 Test, pp. 111-112

EFFECTIVE INSTRUCTION CD
- ❏ Use the Word® file to tailor your own Lesson Plan.
- ❏ Use the **ExamView**® Test Generator to create your own chapter test.

FOCUS

❏ Write the following statement on the board for students to complete: "I am a citizen of _____." Ask students to share their responses and list the different answers on the board. Point out that it is possible to be a citizen of several different groups. Explain that in this chapter they will learn about the rights and responsibilities of citizenship.

TEACH

❏ **Reading.** Have students read text pages 95-106.

❏ **Responsibilities of Citizens.** Brainstorm with students the responsibilities they have as members of a community. These responsibilities might include observing the rules posted at community facilities, cleaning up after pets, and caring for shared public property. Help students understand the reasons communities need responsible citizens.

❏ **Explore Volunteer Opportunities.** Assign the *Explore* activity on page 97. Allow time for students to exchange information about their volunteer experiences.

❏ **Leadership Qualities.** Ask students to work in pairs. Have them write the word *leader* vertically on a blank sheet of paper. Then ask the student pairs to identify characteristics of a good leader, using words that start with each letter of the word. Then have students share their responses with the rest of the class.

(Continued on next page)

Chapter 5 Lesson Plan continued

❏ **Teamwork.** Review the meaning of the word *teamwork* with the class. Then ask students to look through magazines and cut out pictures that illustrate the concept of teamwork. Use the illustrations to create a classroom collage titled "Teamwork Works."

❏ **How to Elect a Classroom Council.** Assign the *How To* activity on page 102. Work with students to determine a suitable date for the election.

❏ **A Closer Look at Citizenship Skills.** Discuss pages 104-105. Ask students to share their reactions to the information provided.

ASSESS

❏ Use the reproducible Chapter 5 Test on page 111 of this *Teacher Resource Guide,* or construct your own test using the **Exam** *View®* Test Generator found on the *Effective Instruction CD-ROM.*

CLOSE

❏ **Chapter 5 Review & Activities.** Have students answer the questions on text page 107.

❏ Ask students to identify some of the ways they can demonstrate citizenship and leadership skills in their everyday life.

Managing Your Life

CHAPTER 6 OBJECTIVES

Students will discover…
- ◆ the importance of making short-term and long-term goals.
- ◆ how to set realistic goals.
- ◆ the difference between routine and major decisions.
- ◆ how to make responsible decisions.

CHAPTER 6 RESOURCES

STUDENT WORKBOOK
- ❏ Worksheet #30 through #35

STUDENT MOTIVATION KIT
Project & Activity Cards
- ❏ #13-14: Go for the Goal

Career Investigation Activities
- ❏ Career Activity #6, 43 & 49

Reteaching Activities
- ❏ Taking One Step at a Time
- ❏ Looking Ahead

Enrichment Activities
- ❏ A Planning Journal

TEACHER RESOURCE GUIDE
- ❏ Chapter 6 Test, pp. 113-114

EFFECTIVE INSTRUCTION CD
- ❏ Use the Word® file to tailor your own Lesson Plan.
- ❏ Use the **Exam**View® Test Generator to create your own chapter test.

FOCUS

- ❏ Ask students to list skills they have tried to master in the last few years, such as learning to skate, or learning to play an instrument. Call on volunteers to share their lists. Point out that the skills they want to master are goals. This chapter explains how to set realistic goals and make decisions.

TEACH

- ❏ **Reading.** Have students read text pages 109-120.
- ❏ **Identifying Goals.** Ask students to create a ten-year time line for goals. Have them draw a horizontal line across a sheet of paper, divide it into ten equal segments, and label each segment with consecutive years, starting with the current year at the far left. Then have them write anticipated goals on their time line, with projected dates for accomplishment. Ask students to circle their three most important goals.
- ❏ **How to Create a Goal-Setting Worksheet.** Assign the *How To* activity on page 113. Draw students' attention to the tips listed under *Check the Facts*.
- ❏ **Consequences.** Organize the class into small groups. Have each group identify a situation in which it would be important to consider the consequences before making a decision. Ask each group to illustrate the situation as a cartoon titled "Think Before You Act." Discuss the completed cartoons.

(Continued on next page)

Chapter 6 Lesson Plan *continued*

❏ **Procrastination.** Write on the board "Never put off till tomorrow what you can do today." Review with students the meaning of procrastination—putting off tasks rather than being disciplined and getting them done. Point out that people often avoid tasks that are boring, difficult, or unpleasant. Ask students to suggest ways to avoid procrastination.

❏ **Explore Decision Making.** Assign the *Explore* activity on page 117. Ask volunteers to describe the decision they made and the alternatives they considered.

❏ **A Closer Look at Decisions.** Discuss pages 118-119. Ask students to share their reactions to the information provided.

ASSESS

❏ Use the reproducible Chapter 6 Test on page 113 of this *Teacher Resource Guide*, or construct your own test using the **Exam***View*® Test Generator found on the *Effective Instruction CD-ROM*.

CLOSE

❏ **Chapter 6 Review & Activities.** Have students answer the questions on text page 121.

❏ Have students list five major decisions they expect to make in the next five years. Ask students to explain how using the decision-making process will help them make those decisions when the time comes.

Chapter 7 Lesson Plan

Exploring Careers

CHAPTER 7 OBJECTIVES

Students will discover...
- considerations for choosing a career.
- why you should plan your career path.
- how to research careers.
- reasons why people work.

CHAPTER 7 RESOURCES

STUDENT WORKBOOK
- ❏ Worksheet #36 through #40

STUDENT MOTIVATION KIT
Project & Activity Cards
- ❏ #15: Seeking Employment
- ❏ #16: Reading Want Ads

Career Investigation Activities
- ❏ Career Activity #8, 9, 10, 11, 12, 13, 14 & 17

Reteaching Activities
- ❏ Career Decisions

Enrichment Activities
- ❏ Young Speakers
- ❏ Finding a Job Match

TEACHER RESOURCE GUIDE
- ❏ Chapter 7 Test, pp. 115-116

EFFECTIVE INSTRUCTION CD
- ❏ Use the Word® file to tailor your own Lesson Plan.
- ❏ Use the **ExamView**® Test Generator to create your own chapter test.

FOCUS

- ❏ Ask students to identify school subjects and recreational activities that they enjoy. List some responses on the board. Then ask students to identify possible jobs that would match some of these school subjects and recreational activities. Point out that this chapter explores ways that personal interests can be matched to careers.

TEACH

- ❏ **Reading.** Have students read text pages 125-138.
- ❏ **Career Exploration.** Ask students to discuss the benefits of career exploration before entering high school. Ask students to identify jobs that are related to the school subjects they are taking. Ask how they can learn which subjects will be helpful in specific careers.
- ❏ **A Closer Look at Researching Jobs.** Discuss pages 128-129. Ask students to share their reactions to the information provided.
- ❏ **How to Figure Education & Training Costs.** Assign the *How To* activity on page 132. Emphasize the importance of researching grants and scholarships.
- ❏ **Apprenticeships.** Invite someone who is in an apprenticeship program to speak to the class. Before the speaker arrives, organize the class into small groups and have students prepare questions to ask the apprentice. Hold a class discussion the following day about the advantages and disadvantages of apprenticeship.

(Continued on next page)

Chapter 7 Lesson Plan *continued*

❏ **Teen Jobs.** Have students brainstorm job possibilities for young teens. Examples could include babysitting, pet-sitting, running errands, and raking leaves. Ask students to explain how a job today can lead to a career tomorrow. How can a part-time job help prepare a teen for the world of work?

❏ **Explore Your Career Interests.** Assign the *Explore* activity on page 135. Have volunteers identify their potential careers.

ASSESS

❏ Use the reproducible Chapter 7 Test on page 115 of this *Teacher Resource Guide*, or construct your own test using the **Exam**_View_® Test Generator found on the *Effective Instruction CD-ROM*.

CLOSE

❏ **Chapter 7 Review & Activities.** Have students answer the questions on text page 139.

❏ Have students complete the following statement: "When I am 21 years old, I want to be _____." Ask students to share their answers and explain their choices.

Chapter 8 Lesson Plan

Employability Skills

CHAPTER 8 OBJECTIVES

Students will discover...
- ◆ how basic skills like reading, writing, math, science, speaking, listening, and technology contribute to success in life.
- ◆ why technology is essential in the workplace.
- ◆ how to apply for a job.
- ◆ how to prepare for a job interview.
- ◆ how you can advance on the job.

CHAPTER 8 RESOURCES

STUDENT WORKBOOK
- ❏ Worksheet #41 through #45

STUDENT MOTIVATION KIT
Project & Activity Cards
- ❏ #17: Practicing Job Interviews
- ❏ #18: Teamwork

Career Investigation Activities
- ❏ Career Activity #2, 3, 7, 15, 16, 18 & 19

Reteaching Activities
- ❏ Writing a Résumé
- ❏ Be an Entrepreneur

Enrichment Activities
- ❏ Interview an Entrepreneur
- ❏ Start Your Own Business

TEACHER RESOURCE GUIDE
- ❏ Chapter 8 Test, pp. 117-118

EFFECTIVE INSTRUCTION CD
- ❏ Use the Word® file to tailor your own Lesson Plan.
- ❏ Use the **Exam***View*® Test Generator to create your own chapter test.

FOCUS

- ❏ Display the following items on a table: a newspaper, a checkbook, a job application, a CD-ROM, a measuring cup, a city map, a telephone. Ask students to write down the kinds of skills—reading, writing, math, science, speaking, listening, technology— that are used with each item. Have students share their responses. Point out that this chapter focuses on the importance of developing basic employability skills for workplace success.

TEACH

- ❏ **Reading.** Have students read text pages 141-156.
- ❏ **Speaking and Listening.** Have student pairs practice speaking and listening skills by role-playing the parts of teacher and student in the following scenario:

  Your math teacher has asked to speak with you about your grades. You've been having difficulty in math class. You have forgotten your homework several times and failed a chapter test.

  Have the partners switch roles, allowing each person to play each role. Then ask the rest of the class to evaluate the conversations, based on how effectively each pair of students used speaking and listening skills.
- ❏ **A Closer Look at a Résumé.** Discuss pages 148-149. Ask students to share their reactions to the information provided.

(Continued on next page)

Chapter 8 Lesson Plan *continued*

❏ **How to Prepare for a Job Interview.**
Have students work in pairs to complete
the *How To* activity on page 150.

❏ **Teamwork.** Point out that individual
work records often include a section on an
employee's teamwork skills. Ask students
to identify behaviors that would help to
strengthen a team, and behaviors that
would weaken it.

❏ **Explore Working in Teams.** Assign the
Explore activity on page 153. Have teams
discuss their experiences after they have
completed the assignment.

ASSESS

❏ Use the reproducible Chapter 8 Test on
page 117 of this *Teacher Resource Guide*, or
construct your own test using the
Exam*View*® Test Generator found on the
Effective Instruction CD-ROM.

CLOSE

❏ **Chapter 8 Review & Activities.**
Have students answer the questions on
text page 157.

❏ Ask students to debate the following
statement: "The way to advance in a job is
to toot your own horn."

Caring for Children

CHAPTER 9 OBJECTIVES

Students will discover...

- ◆ how parenting skills can help you interact positively with children.
- ◆ how infants, toddlers, and preschoolers learn through play.
- ◆ how infants and children develop.
- ◆ what to expect when interacting with infants and children.
- ◆ how to help children learn.

CHAPTER 9 RESOURCES

STUDENT WORKBOOK
❏ Worksheet #46 through #51

STUDENT MOTIVATION KIT
Project & Activity Cards
❏ #19: Growth Charts

Career Investigation Activities
❏ Career Activity #38, 39, 40, 41 & 42

Reteaching Activities
❏ Caring for Children
❏ How Children Learn

Enrichment Activities
❏ Children Can Dress Themselves

TEACHER RESOURCE GUIDE
❏ Chapter 9 Test, pp. 119-120

EFFECTIVE INSTRUCTION CD
❏ Use the Word® file to tailor your own Lesson Plan.
❏ Use the **Exam***View*® Test Generator to create your own chapter test.

FOCUS

❏ Ask students, "What does it mean to be a parent?" Write their responses on the board. Explain that in this chapter they will learn about the qualities and skills necessary for parenting.

TEACH

❏ **Reading.** Have students read text pages 159-176.

❏ **Children's Needs.** Have students create a chart titled "Children's Needs." Use four columns labeled "Physical," Intellectual," "Emotional," and "Social." Have students work in small groups to give examples of each. Ask each group to share their responses.

❏ **Positive Parenting.** Have students work in pairs to create skits about positive parenting. Have one student role-play a child and the other student role-play a caregiver. Have the class watch each pair's skit and discuss how positive parenting is demonstrated.

❏ **Child Abuse.** Emphasize the seriousness of child abuse by pointing to its long-term effects. Explain that many people who are abused continue to experience pain and suffering for many years.

❏ **Children With Special Needs.** Ask students to research and read articles by or about parents of children with special needs. Encourage students to look for ways the parents encourage and motivate their children to become independent. Have students present their findings to the class.

(Continued on next page)

Chapter 9 Lesson Plan continued

❏ **A Closer Look at Child Development.**
Discuss pages 168-169. Ask students to share their reactions to the information provided.

❏ **How to Choose Age-Appropriate Toys.**
Assign the *How To* activity on page 171. Arrange for students to share and compare their findings.

❏ **Explore Quiet Play Activities.**
Assign the *Explore* activity on page 175. Hold a class discussion after students have completed the assignment to determine the most effective quiet play activities.

ASSESS

❏ Use the reproducible Chapter 9 Test on page 119 of this *Teacher Resource Guide,* or construct your own test using the **Exam***View*® Test Generator found on the *Effective Instruction CD-ROM.*

CLOSE

❏ **Chapter 9 Review & Activities.**
Have students answer the questions on text page 177.

❏ Repeat the *Focus* activity. Ask students what they added to their list now that they have studied the chapter.

Babysitting Basics

CHAPTER 10 OBJECTIVES

Students will discover...
- how to keep children safe.
- how to prevent common accidents.
- how to prepare for babysitting jobs.
- how to care for infants, toddlers, and preschoolers.

CHAPTER 10 RESOURCES

STUDENT WORKBOOK
- ❏ Worksheet #52 through #56

STUDENT MOTIVATION KIT
Project & Activity Cards
- ❏ #20: Activity Book
- ❏ #21: Modeling Dough

Career Investigation Activities
- ❏ Career Activity #38 & 40

Reteaching Activities
- ❏ Child Safety
- ❏ Choosing Toys for Children

Enrichment Activities
- ❏ Babysitting Dilemmas
- ❏ Making a Children's Book
- ❏ Bean Bag Toss

TEACHER RESOURCE GUIDE
- ❏ Chapter 10 Test, pp. 121-122

EFFECTIVE INSTRUCTION CD
- ❏ Use the Word® file to tailor your own Lesson Plan.
- ❏ Use the **Exam**_View_® Test Generator to create your own chapter test.

FOCUS

❏ Ask students to share memorable babysitting experiences, such as most difficult, most challenging, and funniest. Point out that babysitting is a big responsibility. Tell students that in this chapter they will learn how to babysit infants, toddlers, and preschoolers.

TEACH

❏ **Reading.** Have students read text pages 179-192.

❏ **Childproofing a Home.** Organize students into small groups and assign each group a room in a home, such as kitchen, bathroom, or bedroom. Ask each group to figure out what needs to be done to childproof the room. Have each group share their list with other groups.

❏ **Babysitting Basics.** Working in small groups, have students develop a pamphlet titled "Before You Babysit." Post the pamphlets in the classroom.

❏ **A Closer Look at Giving a Child CPR.** Discuss pages 182-183. Ask students to share their reactions to the information provided.

❏ **Explore Making a First-Aid Kit.** Assign the _Explore_ activity on page 186.

(Continued on next page)

Chapter 10 Lesson Plan continued

❏ **Babysitter's Bag.** Suggest that students compile their own "Babysitter's Bag" that they can take with them on babysitting jobs. The bag could contain a few inexpensive toys, crayons, storybooks, puppets, and other appropriate items.

❏ **How to Create a Babysitter's Resource Guide.** Assign the *How To* activity on page 188.

ASSESS

❏ Use the reproducible Chapter 10 Test on page 121 of this *Teacher Resource Guide*, or construct your own test using the **Exam** *View*® Test Generator found on the *Effective Instruction CD-ROM*.

CLOSE

❏ **Chapter 10 Review & Activities.** Have students answer the questions on text page 193.

❏ Ask students to complete the following sentence: "When caring for children, a good caregiver _____."

Managing Your Money

CHAPTER 11 OBJECTIVES

Students will discover…
- ◆ how to evaluate advertisements.
- ◆ how to compare price and quality.
- ◆ sources of income and expenses.
- ◆ how to develop a plan for spending and saving money.
- ◆ how to manage your money.

CHAPTER 11 RESOURCES

STUDENT WORKBOOK
❏ Worksheet #57 through #62

STUDENT MOTIVATION KIT
Project & Activity Cards
❏ #22: Consumer Letter
❏ #23: Budgeting Game

Career Investigation Activities
❏ Career Activity #43, 44, 45 & 46

Reteaching Activities
❏ Influences on Consumer Choices
❏ Media Messages
❏ Your Consumer Rights
❏ Making Good Consumer Choices
❏ Being a Wise Consumer

Enrichment Activities
❏ Rally Around Your Rights
❏ Ads—Fact or Fantasy
❏ Compare & Save
❏ Buying Choices

TEACHER RESOURCE GUIDE
❏ Chapter 11 Test, pp. 123-124

EFFECTIVE INSTRUCTION CD
❏ Use the Word® file to tailor your own Lesson Plan.
❏ Use the **ExamView**® Test Generator to create your own chapter test.

FOCUS

❏ Make a chart with the following headings: Peers, Parents, Teachers, Siblings, Salespeople. Ask students to think of a major item they would like to purchase, and identify three people they would ask for advice before making their purchase. Have them share their responses. Tally students' responses on the chart. Point out that in this chapter they will learn about the many influences on their buying decisions.

TEACH

❏ **Reading.** Have students read text pages 195-216.

❏ **Ads for Teens.** Organize students into small groups and provide each group with a popular teen magazine. Ask groups to calculate the percentage of space devoted to ads, and discuss whether the ads in the magazines influence their buying decisions. Ask each group to identify three ads that they think might strongly influence teens. Have each group explain its choices to the class.

❏ **A Closer Look at Types of Media.** Discuss pages 200-201. Ask students to share their reactions to the information provided.

❏ **Explore Consumer Reports Magazine.** Assign the *Explore* activity on page 207. Hold a class discussion to compare findings after students have completed the assignment.

❏ **Consumer Rights.** Have students describe instances in which they felt that their consumer rights were violated. Discuss what recourse the students had in each situation.

(Continued on next page)

Chapter 11 Lesson Plan continued

❏ **Managing Money.** Write the following statements on the board:

A. A penny saved is a penny earned.

B. Save for a rainy day.

C. Penny wise, pound foolish.

Ask students what the statements mean. Emphasize that the teen years are the time to develop good money management skills.

❏ **How to Recognize Your Expenses.** After students complete the *How To* activity on page 215, ask volunteers to share what they learned from the exercise.

ASSESS

❏ Use the reproducible Chapter 11 Test on page 123 of this *Teacher Resource Guide*, or construct your own test using the **Exam***View*® Test Generator found on the *Effective Instruction CD-ROM*.

CLOSE

❏ **Chapter 11 Review & Activities.** Have students answer the questions on text page 217.

❏ Ask students to identify one aspect of their buying habits that they would change as a result of reading this chapter.

Chapter 12
Lesson Plan

Managing Your Resources

CHAPTER 12 OBJECTIVES

Students will discover…
- ◆ the management process.
- ◆ personal, material, and community resources to help you reach your goals.
- ◆ time-management tools and techniques.
- ◆ how to improve your study skills.
- ◆ the effects of stress.

CHAPTER 12 RESOURCES

STUDENT WORKBOOK
❑ Worksheet #63 through #67

STUDENT MOTIVATION KIT
Project & Activity Cards
❑ #24: Managing Your Money
❑ #25-26: Car Organizer
Career Investigation Activities
❑ Career Activity #47, 48 & 49
Reteaching Activities
❑ Scheduling Time
Enrichment Activities
❑ A Soothing Bath Mix

TEACHER RESOURCE GUIDE
❑ Chapter 12 Test, pp. 125-126

EFFECTIVE INSTRUCTION CD
❑ Use the Word® file to tailor your own Lesson Plan.
❑ Use the **Exam***View*® Test Generator to create your own chapter test.

FOCUS

❑ Ask for a show of hands to indicate the number of students who feel that they never have enough time to do all that they need to get done. Point out that time, just like other resources, needs to be managed. Explain that in this chapter they will learn skills that they can use to manage time and other resources.

TEACH

❑ **Reading.** Have students read text pages 219-232.
❑ **The Management Process.** Have students list some areas of their life that could be improved through better management. Suggest that they choose one area, and use the steps of the management process to plan, do, and evaluate the activity. Ask volunteers to describe how they plan to use the management process and predict how it will make a difference.
❑ **Time Management.** Help students rate their time management skills by having them answer the following questions:
  A. Are you almost always in a hurry?
  B. Do you often fail to finish tasks?
  C. Do you feel that you are working hard but not accomplishing much?
  D. Are you regularly late with assignments?
  E. Do you often try to do several things at once?
  F. Do you have trouble deciding what to do next?

(Continued on next page)

Chapter 12 Lesson Plan continued

Tell students that if most of their answers were *yes,* they should use the techniques discussed in this chapter to make better use of their time.

❏ **Management Tools.** Point out that cell phones, PDAs, and computer notepads are designed to help people manage their lives more effectively. Have students interview someone who uses one of these devices as a management tool. Ask students to report their findings to the class, then have students draw conclusions.

❏ **How to Create a Schedule of Activities.** Assign the *How To* activity on page 226. Ask volunteers to share some of their conclusions.

❏ **Explore Reducing Stress.** Assign the *Explore* activity on page 229. Hold a classroom discussion on the connection between over-scheduling and stress.

❏ **A Closer Look at Handling Stress.** Discuss pages 230-231. Ask students to share their reactions to the information provided.

ASSESS

❏ Use the reproducible Chapter 12 Test on page 125 of this *Teacher Resource Guide,* or construct your own test using the **Exam***View*® Test Generator found on the *Effective Instruction CD-ROM.*

CLOSE

❏ **Chapter 12 Review & Activities.** Have students answer the questions on text page 233.

❏ Have students prepare a list of changes they plan to make in the way they manage their resources and time as a result of reading this chapter.

Your Living Space

CHAPTER 13 OBJECTIVES

Students will discover…
- how a home provides shelter and security.
- how to organize and share your living space.
- how design elements and principles are used.
- the value of keeping your home clean and safe.

CHAPTER 13 RESOURCES

STUDENT WORKBOOK
❏ Worksheet #68 through #73

STUDENT MOTIVATION KIT
Project & Activity Cards
❏ #27: Designing & Organizing
❏ #28: Message Board
Career Investigation Activities
❏ Career Activity #52, 53, 54 & 55
Reteaching Activities
❏ Design a Room
Enrichment Activities
❏ Homes of All Kinds

TEACHER RESOURCE GUIDE
❏ Chapter 13 Test, pp. 127-128

EFFECTIVE INSTRUCTION CD
❏ Use the Word® file to tailor your own Lesson Plan.
❏ Use the **Exam**View® Test Generator to create your own chapter test.

FOCUS

❏ Display a picture of a well-decorated room. Ask students to write down three features of the room that catch their eye. Discuss student responses, and introduce the concepts of space, shape, line, texture, and color. Explain that in this chapter they will learn about the many design elements that go into creating a living space.

TEACH

❏ **Reading.** Have students read text pages 235-252.

❏ **Evaluating Space.** Have students work in small groups to evaluate the way the classroom is organized. Ask them to consider storage, traffic patterns, and so on. Students should identify parts of the room that could use improvement. Have them sketch out their ideas for improvement and present their ideas to the class.

❏ **How to Create a Floor Plan.** Assign the *How To* activity on page 238.

❏ **Design Elements.** Have students think about how they would like to change a room in their home. Tell them to make two plans for changing the room. In the first plan they should change only one design element, such as color. In the second plan, they should change two or more elements. They might add furniture with different lines, or pillows for texture. Suggest that students make "before" and "after" pictures of their room.

(Continued on next page)

Chapter 13 Lesson Plan *continued*

❏ **Special Needs.** Discuss the housing needs of people with physical challenges. Consider these issues: getting into and out of the home; moving from room to room; using kitchen facilities; using bathroom facilities; and so on. Have students find out what equipment is available to help physically-challenged people, and how homes can be adapted to their needs.

❏ **Home Safety.** As a class, prepare a checklist that could be used to inspect homes for hazards. Suggest that students use the checklist at home, discuss any hazards they find with family members, and suggest ways to correct the hazards.

❏ **A Closer Look at Closet Organization.** Discuss pages 240-241. Ask students to share their reactions to the information provided.

❏ **Explore Planning an Escape Route.** Assign the *Explore* activity on page 250.

ASSESS

❏ Use the reproducible Chapter 13 Test on page 127 of this *Teacher Resource Guide*, or construct your own test using the **Exam** *View*® Test Generator found on the *Effective Instruction CD-ROM*.

CLOSE

❏ **Chapter 13 Review & Activities.** Have students answer the questions on text page 253.

❏ Ask students to write a short essay about how they will design their living space for comfort and safety.

Chapter 14
Lesson Plan

Your Environment

CHAPTER 14 OBJECTIVES

Students will discover...
- ◆ the natural resources that make up the environment.
- ◆ ways to conserve natural resources.
- ◆ ways to use energy wisely.
- ◆ what it means to reduce, reuse, and recycle waste.
- ◆ why personal safety is important.

CHAPTER 14 RESOURCES

STUDENT WORKBOOK
- ❏ Worksheet #74 through #78

STUDENT MOTIVATION KIT
Project & Activity Cards
- ❏ #29: Preserving the Environment
- ❏ #30: Garden Stepping Stones

Career Investigation Activities
- ❏ Career Activity #56, 57, 58 & 59

Reteaching Activities
- ❏ Using Resources Responsibly
- ❏ Wise Recycling

Enrichment Activities
- ❏ Votive Candleholders

TEACHER RESOURCE GUIDE
- ❏ Chapter 14 Test, pp. 129-130

EFFECTIVE INSTRUCTION CD
- ❏ Use the Word® file to tailor your own Lesson Plan.
- ❏ Use the **ExamView**® Test Generator to create your own chapter test.

FOCUS

- ❏ Write the word *conservation* on the board and explain that it is one of the main keys to protecting the environment. Ask students to give examples of conservation measures they already practice. Point out that in this chapter they will find out why conservation is so important and what measures they can take to conserve resources.

TEACH

- ❏ **Reading.** Have students read text pages 255-270.
- ❏ **Nuclear Power.** Discuss with students the problem of disposing of hazardous waste. Ask students to find out how it has been handled in the past, what current practices are, and what is planned for the future.
- ❏ **Overpackaging.** Set up a classroom display of common grocery items in various kinds of packaging. Have students determine which items fit into a program that avoids unnecessary packaging. Then ask them to suggest alternative ways of packaging those products.
- ❏ **Reusing Everyday Objects.** Bring to class an assortment of items that might normally be thrown away, such as a coffee can, an egg carton, a cardboard tube from paper towels, and a plastic soda bottle. Challenge small groups to come up with creative ways to reuse each item. Groups should then share their ideas with the entire class.

(Continued on next page)

Chapter 14 Lesson Plan *continued*

❏ **A Closer Look at American Waste.**
Discuss pages 262-263. Ask students to share their reactions to the information provided.

❏ **Explore Recycling.** Assign the *Explore* activity on page 266. Have a volunteer tally students' lists to determine how many items were recycled by students' families in one month.

❏ **How to Recognize Edible Plants.**
Assign the *How To* activity on page 269. Hold a classroom discussion in which students can share their findings.

ASSESS

❏ Use the reproducible Chapter 14 Test on page 129 of this *Teacher Resource Guide,* or construct your own test using the **Exam***View*® Test Generator found on the *Effective Instruction CD-ROM.*

CLOSE

❏ **Chapter 14 Review & Activities.**
Have students answer the questions on text page 271.

❏ Have students create a classroom collage titled "Reduce, Reuse, Recycle" that illustrates many different conservation methods.

Chapter 15 Lesson Plan

Your Fashion Statement

CHAPTER 15 OBJECTIVES

Students will discover…
- ◆ the differences among fashions, fads, and classic styles.
- ◆ how the color, line, and texture of clothing affect your appearance.
- ◆ how to assess your wardrobe needs.
- ◆ how accessories can stretch your wardrobe.

CHAPTER 15 RESOURCES

STUDENT WORKBOOK
- ❏ Worksheet #79 through #84

STUDENT MOTIVATION KIT
Project & Activity Cards
- ❏ #31: Show Your Style
- ❏ #32: A Color Wheel

Career Investigation Activities
- ❏ Career Activity #60, 62 & 63

Reteaching Activities
- ❏ Using the Color Wheel
- ❏ Clothing Terms

Enrichment Activities
- ❏ Dressing for the Occasion

TEACHER RESOURCE GUIDE
- ❏ Chapter 15 Test, pp. 131-132

EFFECTIVE INSTRUCTION CD
- ❏ Use the Word® file to tailor your own Lesson Plan.
- ❏ Use the **ExamView**® Test Generator to create your own chapter test.

FOCUS

- ❏ Write the following question on the board: "What is your favorite outfit and why do you like it?" Have volunteers share their responses. Survey the class to find out how many students like an outfit because of its color, because they feel good in it, because it makes them look good, and so on. Explain that in this chapter they will learn how to consider design elements when choosing clothes so that they will look their best.

TEACH

- ❏ **Reading.** Have students read text pages 275-290.
- ❏ **Fashions and Fads.** Ask students to work in small groups to find magazine pictures that show classic styles, fashions, and fads. Have groups share their pictures with the class and explain why they placed the pictures in the different categories.
- ❏ **Color Basics.** Help students understand the meanings of value, tint, and shade with this demonstration. Show them some primary blue poster paint. Add a small amount of black paint to the blue, and ask students what changed. Then mix a little white paint with a sample of blue, and ask what changed. Then ask which of the blues is a tint and which is a shade.

(Continued on next page)

Chapter 15 Lesson Plan *continued*

❏ **The Color Wheel.** Have students use a paint program on a computer to create a color wheel. Before students start, review how green is made *(equal parts of yellow and blue)*. Then ask how they would make yellow-green and blue-green *(add more yellow to make yellow-green and add more blue to make blue-green)*.

❏ **Clothing Lines.** Have small groups of students find examples of clothing that shows vertical, horizontal, and diagonal lines. Ask them to place tracing paper over the pictures and trace the lines in the clothing pictures. Have them label the lines in each garment and explain their line tracings to the class.

❏ **A Closer Look at Mixing & Matching.** Discuss pages 278-279. Ask students to share their reactions to the information provided.

❏ **Explore a Wardrobe Inventory.** Assign the *Explore* activity on page 287. Brainstorm with students ways to recycle clothes that they no longer wear.

❏ **How to Tie Scarves & Neckties.** Have students work in pairs to complete the *How To* activity on page 289.

ASSESS

❏ Use the reproducible Chapter 15 Test on page 131 of this *Teacher Resource Guide*, or construct your own test using the **Exam***View*® Test Generator found on the *Effective Instruction CD-ROM*.

CLOSE

❏ **Chapter 15 Review & Activities.** Have students answer the questions on text page 291.

❏ Ask students to write a paragraph explaining how knowing the effects of color, line, and texture can help them make the best clothing selections.

Clothing Basics

CHAPTER 16 OBJECTIVES

Students will discover...
- how to recognize quality in clothing.
- how to develop a shopping plan.
- what clothing labels tell you.
- how to remove stains from clothing.
- guidelines for washing, drying, and ironing clothes.
- how to store clothes properly.

CHAPTER 16 RESOURCES

STUDENT WORKBOOK
- ❏ Worksheet #85 through #89

STUDENT MOTIVATION KIT
Project & Activity Cards
- ❏ #33: Fashion Report
- ❏ #34: Comparing Natural Fibers

Career Investigation Activities
- ❏ Career Activity #60 & 64

Reteaching Activities
- ❏ Wise Clothes Shopping
- ❏ Planning Your Wardrobe
- ❏ What's It Really Worth?

Enrichment Activities
- ❏ Getting the Most for Your Money

TEACHER RESOURCE GUIDE
- ❏ Chapter 16 Test, pp. 133-134

EFFECTIVE INSTRUCTION CD
- ❏ Use the Word® file to tailor your own Lesson Plan.
- ❏ Use the **ExamView**® Test Generator to create your own chapter test.

FOCUS

- ❏ Write the following sentence on the board for students to complete: "I think that _____ are the best brand of jeans because _____." Have students share their responses and discuss the factors that help determine the best choice. Point out that in this chapter they will learn how to judge quality, spend their clothing dollars wisely, and take care of their clothes.

TEACH

- ❏ **Reading.** Have students read text pages 293-310.
- ❏ **Fabric Construction.** Provide fabric swatches so students can examine weaves. Have students separate the threads so that they can see the way lengthwise and crosswise threads are interlaced. Have them unravel a thread to examine the fibers. Students might sketch and label what they observe.
- ❏ **Explore Natural Dyes.** Assign the *Explore* activity on page 296. Allow classroom time for students to compare their findings.
- ❏ **Catalog Shopping.** Provide students with clothing catalogs and have them choose an item they would like to purchase. Then, ask them to find information about fabric, style, quality of construction, and cleaning information for that item. Have students evaluate the catalogs in terms of the information they provide.

(Continued on next page)

Chapter 16 Lesson Plan continued

❏ **Shopping Hints.** Ask students to write a "Shopping Hints" article for the school paper. Articles should explain why such factors as quality, style, budget, where to shop, and method of payment must be considered when making a shopping plan.

❏ **Clothing Care.** Ask students to work in small groups to create a commercial that illustrates the guidelines for proper care of clothes. Students should include the information presented in the chapter. Ask groups to present their commercials to the class.

❏ **A Closer Look at Quality Construction.** Discuss pages 300-301. Ask students to share their reactions to the information provided.

❏ **How to Remove Stains.** Assign the *How To* activity on page 308. Have students report on the success of their efforts.

ASSESS

❏ Use the reproducible Chapter 16 Test on page 133 of this *Teacher Resource Guide*, or construct your own test using the **Exam***View*® Test Generator found on the *Effective Instruction CD-ROM*.

CLOSE

❏ **Chapter 16 Review & Activities.** Have students answer the questions on text page 311.

❏ Ask students to write a paragraph describing two things they will do differently before shopping for clothes again.

Chapter 17 Lesson Plan

Preparing to Sew

CHAPTER 17 OBJECTIVES

Students will discover...
- ◆ how to operate a sewing machine.
- ◆ what to look for when choosing a sewing project.
- ◆ how to determine your correct pattern size.
- ◆ how to select the best fabric for your sewing project.

CHAPTER 17 RESOURCES

STUDENT WORKBOOK
- ❏ Worksheet #90 through #94

STUDENT MOTIVATION KIT
Project & Activity Cards
- ❏ #35: Fabrics & Their Uses

Career Investigation Activities
- ❏ Career Activity #51 & 60

Reteaching Activities
- ❏ Fabric Makes the Difference
- ❏ Choosing a Pattern

Enrichment Activities
- ❏ Fabric Swatch Book

TEACHER RESOURCE GUIDE
- ❏ Chapter 17 Test, pp. 135-136

EFFECTIVE INSTRUCTION CD
- ❏ Use the Word® file to tailor your own Lesson Plan.
- ❏ Use the **Exam***View*® Test Generator to create your own chapter test.

FOCUS

- ❏ Ask students to think of sewing projects they would like to undertake. List their ideas on the board and discuss the different fabrics, notions, and skills that would be needed for different projects. Explain that in this chapter they will learn what to look for when choosing a sewing project.

TEACH

- ❏ **Reading.** Have students read text pages 313-326.
- ❏ **How to Use a Sewing Machine.** Assign the *How To* activity on page 316. Allow time for students to compare stitch samples.
- ❏ **Comparing Sewing Machines.** Have students research various brands of sewing machines. Ask them to develop a chart to compare the costs, features, and durability among three brands. Have students choose the machine that they believe is the best buy and give reasons for their choice.
- ❏ **Pattern Envelopes.** Have students study the front and back of a pattern envelope. Ask them to answer the following questions about the envelope:

    A. How many views of the garment are shown?
    B. How is the garment described?
    C. How much fabric is needed for the smallest size?
    D. How much fabric is needed for the largest size?
    E. What fabrics are recommended?
    F. What notions are required?

(Continued on next page)

Chapter 17 Lesson Plan continued

❏ **A Closer Look at Small Sewing Tools.**
Discuss pages 320-321. Ask students to share
their reactions to the information provided.

❏ **Explore Making a Sewing Kit.** Assign
the *Explore* activity on page 325.

ASSESS

❏ Use the reproducible Chapter 17 Test on
page 135 of this *Teacher Resource Guide,* or
construct your own test using the
ExamView® Test Generator found on the
Effective Instruction CD-ROM.

CLOSE

❏ **Chapter 17 Review & Activities.**
Have students answer the questions on
text page 327.

❏ Discuss the following saying with the class:
"A stitch in time saves nine."

Name_____ Date_____ Class _____

Sewing & Serging Basics

CHAPTER 18 OBJECTIVES

Students will discover…
◆ how to prepare your fabric and use a pattern guide sheet.
◆ how to check pattern pieces and measurements.
◆ the basics of machine sewing.
◆ hand-sewing techniques.
◆ how a serger works.
◆ how to make basic repairs and alterations.

CHAPTER 18 RESOURCES

STUDENT WORKBOOK
❏ Worksheet #95 through #99

STUDENT MOTIVATION KIT
Project & Activity Cards
❏ #36: Stitching Techniques
Sewing Labs
❏ Project #1 through #16
Career Investigation Activities
❏ Career Activity #37, 60 & 65
Reteaching Activities
❏ Sewing Machine Basics
❏ Common Serger Stitches
Enrichment Activities
❏ Pattern Layout Mistakes

TEACHER RESOURCE GUIDE
❏ Chapter 18 Test, pp. 137-138

EFFECTIVE INSTRUCTION CD
❏ Use the Word® file to tailor your own Lesson Plan.
❏ Use the **ExamView**® Test Generator to create your own chapter test.

FOCUS

❏ Have students read the opening paragraph on page 329. Ask them to suggest what Evan must do before he starts sewing. Point out that preparation is the key to success in all sewing projects. Explain that in this chapter they will learn how to make simple items and how to make basic repairs.

TEACH

❏ **Reading.** Have students read text pages 329-350.

❏ **Pattern Guide Sheets.** Organize students into small groups and give each group a different guide sheet. Encourage students to study the guide sheets closely and identify the kind of information provided. Then have groups exchange guide sheets and then repeat the exercise until all groups have studied all guide sheets. After groups have made their comparisons, ask: Which guide sheet provided the most information? Which one would you prefer to use and why?

❏ **Pinning Pattern Pieces.** Have students make a flow chart showing the steps involved in pinning pattern pieces. Ask them to number the steps.

❏ **Easing.** One of the more difficult sewing tasks for students to master is the technique of easing fabric. Show them how to push and bend the easing fabric into position as you stitch a seam. Allow students ample time to practice this task.

❏ **How to Make a T-Shirt.** Assign the *How To* activity on page 341. Arrange for volunteers to model their completed T-shirts.

(Continued on next page)

Chapter 18 Lesson Plan *continued*

❏ **A Closer Look at Hand-Sewing Techniques.** Discuss pages 342-343. Ask students to share their reactions to the information provided.

❏ **Serged Seams.** Have students examine the clothing in their home closets to try to find an example of a serged seam.

❏ **Explore Serging Stitches.** Assign the *Explore* activity on page 348. Discuss the advantages of having stitch samples on hand when using a serger.

ASSESS

❏ Use the reproducible Chapter 18 Test on page 137 of this *Teacher Resource Guide*, or construct your own test using the **Exam***View*® Test Generator found on the *Effective Instruction CD-ROM*.

CLOSE

❏ **Chapter 18 Review & Activities.** Have students answer the questions on text page 351.

❏ Have students write a few sentences explaining why it is important to know how to sew by hand.

Expressing Creativity

CHAPTER 19 OBJECTIVES

Students will discover…
◆ how art allows you to express yourself.
◆ ways to create wearable art.
◆ how to use creativity to decorate.

CHAPTER 19 RESOURCES

STUDENT WORKBOOK
❏ Worksheet #100 through #103

STUDENT MOTIVATION KIT
Project & Activity Cards
❏ #37-38: Ribbon Bookmark
❏ #39-40: Recycling Denim Jeans
Foods Labs
❏ Lab #10, 12, 13, 15 & 21
Sewing Labs
❏ Project #1 through #16
Career Investigation Activities
❏ Activity #29 & 33
Reteaching Activities
❏ Recycling Clothes
Enrichment Activities
❏ Appliqué Shirt
❏ Fabric Wall Hanging

TEACHER RESOURCE GUIDE
❏ Chapter 19 Test, pp. 139-140

EFFECTIVE INSTRUCTION CD
❏ Use the Word® file to tailor your own Lesson Plan.
❏ Use the **Exam**View® Test Generator to create your own chapter test.

FOCUS

❏ Point out that people express their creativity in many different ways, and ask volunteers to show examples of creativity. For example, students may show creativity in their hairstyles, clothing, jewelry, and so on. Explain that in this chapter they will discover many different ways of expressing creativity.

TEACH

❏ **Reading.** Have students read text pages 353-362.
❏ **Clothing Concepts.** Ask students if they think teens are more creative in their clothing than any other age group. Discuss reasons why this might be so.
❏ **Button Art.** Bring an assortment of buttons to class and distribute them among groups of students. Challenge groups to come up with as many different ways of using the buttons to create wearable art as they can within five minutes. Remind students that buttons can be stitched or glued onto clothing or accessories. After groups share their ideas and have the class vote on the most creative idea.
❏ **How to Personalize a T-Shirt.** Assign the *How To* activity on page 356. Arrange for volunteers to model their completed T-shirts.
❏ **Creativity with Photos.** Discuss creative ways to use photographs to decorate a room. Ask volunteers to describe the most creative uses of photos that they have seen. Encourage students to discuss the advantages and disadvantages of digital cameras.

(Continued on next page)

Chapter 19 Lesson Plan continued

❏ **Personalizing Living Space.** Tell students to imagine that they have been given a small bedroom to decorate. Ask them to sketch how they would personalize the room, spending no more than $25 on supplies. Display the sketches.

❏ **A Closer Look at Decorative Storage.** Discuss pages 358-359. Ask students to share their reactions to the information provided.

❏ **Explore Faux Finishes.** Assign the *Explore* activity on page 361.

ASSESS

❏ Use the reproducible Chapter 19 Test on page 139 of this *Teacher Resource Guide*, or construct your own test using the **Exam***View®* Test Generator found on the *Effective Instruction CD-ROM*.

CLOSE

❏ **Chapter 19 Review & Activities.** Have students answer the questions on text page 363.

❏ Discuss with students the health benefits of having a creative outlet. Ask volunteers to describe how creativity has helped them deal with different kinds of emotions.

Nutrition & Wellness

CHAPTER 20 OBJECTIVES

Students will discover…
- the difference between hunger and appetite.
- the functions of proteins, carbohydrates, and fats in the human body.
- the functions of vitamins, minerals, and water in the human body.
- the Food Guide Pyramid.
- how Dietary Guidelines promote health.
- the importance of limiting fat, sugar, and salt in the diet.

CHAPTER 20 RESOURCES

STUDENT WORKBOOK
- ❏ Worksheet #104 through #110

STUDENT MOTIVATION KIT
Project & Activity Cards
- ❏ #41: Recipe Cards
- ❏ #42: "Drink Milk"

Career Investigation Activities
- ❏ Career Activity #74, 75, 76 & 77

Reteaching Activities
- ❏ Nutrition Knowledge
- ❏ The Food Guide Pyramid
- ❏ Developing Healthy Habits
- ❏ Sources of Vitamins & Minerals

Enrichment Activities
- ❏ Eating Well
- ❏ Nutrients Around the Globe
- ❏ Looking Out for Fats
- ❏ Guidelines for Vegetarians

TEACHER RESOURCE GUIDE
- ❏ Chapter 20 Test, pp. 141-142

EFFECTIVE INSTRUCTION CD
- ❏ Use the Word® file to tailor your own Lesson Plan.
- ❏ Use the **ExamView**® Test Generator to create your own chapter test.

FOCUS

- ❏ Write the following sentence starters on the board and ask students to complete them: "I should include more _____ in my diet because _____." and "I should eat less _____ because _____." Explain that in this chapter they will learn more about making healthy food choices.

TEACH

- ❏ **Reading.** Have students read text pages 367-388.
- ❏ **Serving Sizes.** To help students better visualize the portion sizes discussed in this chapter, pass around a tennis ball. Discuss whether the servings they eat are larger, smaller, or about the same size as the tennis ball.
- ❏ **Nutrition Through the Life Span.** Point out that people need to pay attention to nutrition throughout the life span. Older people need the same nutrients as teens and younger adults. The amount of food needed tends to decrease in the later years however. Discuss what other menu changes occur as people get older.
- ❏ **Vegetarian Meals.** Have students find recipes for vegetarian dishes. Ask them to plan a vegetarian menu for one day and share it with the class.
- ❏ **A Closer Look at Portion Sizes.** Discuss pages 380-381. Ask students to share their reactions to the information provided.
- ❏ **Explore Healthful Snacks.** Assign the *Explore* activity on page 385.

(Continued on next page)

Chapter 20 Lesson Plan *continued*

❏ **Fast Foods.** Have students work in small groups to analyze a fast food menu. Ask students to determine how they could avoid getting too much fat when eating at a fast food restaurant.

❏ **How to Plan a Balanced Meal.** Assign the *How To* activity on page 387. Allow classroom time for students to discuss their findings.

ASSESS

❏ Use the reproducible Chapter 20 Test on page 141 of this *Teacher Resource Guide,* or construct your own test using the **Exam***View*® Test Generator found on the *Effective Instruction CD-ROM.*

CLOSE

❏ **Chapter 20 Review & Activities.** Have students answer the questions on text page 389.

❏ Ask students to name the five food groups, tell their position on the Food Guide Pyramid, and summarize the major nutrients found in each group.

Health & Fitness

CHAPTER 21 OBJECTIVES

Students will discover...
◆ why health and fitness are important.
◆ how exercise can help you stay healthy and fit.
◆ what you can do to maintain a healthy body weight.
◆ how eating disorders can destroy your health.

CHAPTER 21 RESOURCES

STUDENT WORKBOOK
❏ Worksheet #111 through #115

STUDENT MOTIVATION KIT
Project & Activity Cards
❏ #43: Fitness Video
❏ #44: Health Tips Brochure
Career Investigation Activities
❏ Career Activity #74, 75 & 78
Reteaching Activities
❏ Exercise & Fitness
❏ Eating Disorders & Body Image
Enrichment Activities
❏ Heart-Healthy Recipes & Card Holder

TEACHER RESOURCE GUIDE
❏ Chapter 21 Test, pp. 143-144

EFFECTIVE INSTRUCTION CD
❏ Use the Word® file to tailor your own Lesson Plan.
❏ Use the **Exam***View*® Test Generator to create your own chapter test.

FOCUS

❏ Ask students to consider their own level of fitness and rate it on a scale of 1 (unfit) to 10 (extremely fit). Point out that this chapter explores the relationship between exercise and physical fitness, and explains healthy ways of managing weight.

TEACH

❏ **Reading.** Have students read text pages 391-402.

❏ **Regular Exercise.** Emphasize the importance of *regular* exercise. Ask students to name physical activities that they enjoy. List the activities on the board and ask which promote fitness. Lead a class discussion to determine which combinations of activities would enable students to get regular exercise year round.

❏ **Eating Disorders.** Emphasize that eating disorders are psychological problems that are often associated with low self-esteem. Ask students to research eating disorders. Ask students to discuss their findings.

❏ **A Closer Look at Exercise.** Discuss pages 394-395. Ask students to share their reactions to the information provided.

❏ **Explore Heart-Healthy Menus.** Assign the *Explore* activity on page 398. Emphasize that regular exercise is important in keeping the heart healthy.

(Continued on next page)

Chapter 21 Lesson Plan continued

❏ **Weight Management.** Point out that a person who starts jogging for 20 minutes a day, and does it seven days a week for one year would lose more than 20 pounds without reducing his or her intake of food. Discuss the misconception that increased physical activity causes an increase in appetite too.

❏ **How to Design a Workout.** Assign the *How To* activity on page 401.

ASSESS

❏ Use the reproducible Chapter 21 Test on page 143 of this *Teacher Resource Guide*, or construct your own test using the **Exam***View*® Test Generator found on the *Effective Instruction CD-ROM*.

CLOSE

❏ **Chapter 21 Review & Activities.** Have students answer the questions on text page 403.

❏ Ask students to list five benefits of making regular exercise part of their routine.

Working in the Kitchen

CHAPTER 22 OBJECTIVES

Students will discover...

◆ the sources of food contamination.

◆ how to handle food safely.

◆ ways to keep the kitchen clean.

◆ the causes of common kitchen accidents.

◆ ways to prevent common kitchen accidents from occurring.

CHAPTER 22 RESOURCES

STUDENT WORKBOOK
❏ Worksheet #116 through #120

STUDENT MOTIVATION KIT
Project & Activity Cards
❏ #45: Critic's Corner
❏ #46: Kitchen Safety Poster

Foods Labs
❏ Lab #14

Career Investigation Activities
❏ Career Activity #83, 85 & 86

Reteaching Activities
❏ Safety in the Kitchen
❏ Accident Prevention in the Kitchen

Enrichment Activities
❏ First Aid for Burns
❏ Kitchen Safety Practices
❏ Foodborne Illness

TEACHER RESOURCE GUIDE
❏ Chapter 22 Test, pp. 145-146

EFFECTIVE INSTRUCTION CD
❏ Use the Word® file to tailor your own Lesson Plan.
❏ Use the **ExamView**® Test Generator to create your own chapter test.

FOCUS

❏ Point out that more accidents occur in the kitchen than in any other room in the house. Ask students to suggest reasons for this and list their ideas on the board. Explain that in this chapter they will learn how to prevent accidents in the kitchen, as well as ways to prevent food contamination.

TEACH

❏ **Reading.** Have students read text pages 405-418.

❏ **Preventing Contamination.** On a table in the classroom display several items that can cause food contamination and several foods that spoil easily. The items might include a cutting board and a kitchen towel. The food items might include eggs, mayonnaise, and chicken. Discuss with students the proper handling of each item to prevent food contamination.

❏ **The Accident Chain.** Point out that accidents often happen as the result of a pattern of five elements known as the accident chain. On the board, draw a chain with five links. Inside each link write, in order, the following elements: *situation; unsafe habit; unsafe act; accident; results of accident.* Have students choose an unsafe kitchen practice to illustrate the elements of the accident chain. Then explain that most kitchen accidents can be prevented if any one of the first three elements of the chain is changed.

(Continued on next page)

Chapter 22 Lesson Plan *continued*

❏ **Safe Work Habits.** Have volunteers role-play the kitchen safety rules in the following situations:
   A. Washing sharp objects.
   B. Using a knife and cutting board to cut vegetables.
   C. Removing hot dishes from an oven.
   D. Picking up broken glass.

❏ **How to Chop, Slice, Dice & Mince.** Assign the *How To* activity on page 411. Carefully supervise students to see they use the correct cutting methods.

❏ **A Closer Look at Kitchen Tools & Cookware.** Discuss pages 414-415. Ask students to share their reactions to the information provided.

❏ **Explore Napkin Folding.** After students complete the *Explore* activity on page 417, arrange a classroom display of folded napkins.

ASSESS

❏ Use the reproducible Chapter 22 Test on page 145 of this *Teacher Resource Guide*, or construct your own test using the **Exam***View*® Test Generator found on the *Effective Instruction CD-ROM*.

CLOSE

❏ **Chapter 22 Review & Activities.** Have students answer the questions on text page 419.

❏ Ask students to identify three safety issues in their kitchen at home that they will address with family members. Have them explain how they will make their kitchen safer.

Preparing to Cook

CHAPTER 23 OBJECTIVES

Students will discover...
◆ how to plan meals.
◆ why it is helpful to plan before you shop for food.
◆ how to store foods safely.
◆ how to follow different recipe formats.
◆ the meanings of recipe terms and abbreviations.

CHAPTER 23 RESOURCES

STUDENT WORKBOOK
❏ Worksheet #121 through #126

STUDENT MOTIVATION KIT
Project & Activity Cards
❏ #47: Shopping for the Best Buys
❏ #48: What's to Eat?

Foods Labs
❏ Lab #1, 2, 3, 4, 5, 6, 7, 8, 9, 10, 11, 16, 17, 18, 19, 20, 21, 22, 23 & 27

Career Investigation Activities
❏ Career Activity #67, 76 & 77

Reteaching Activities
❏ Buying Food
❏ Cooking Terms
❏ Food Storage Safety Guidelines

Enrichment Activities
❏ Menu-Planning Decisions
❏ Dried Fruit Hangers
❏ Global Food Terms

TEACHER RESOURCE GUIDE
❏ Chapter 23 Test, pp. 147-148

EFFECTIVE INSTRUCTION CD
❏ Use the Word® file to tailor your own Lesson Plan.
❏ Use the **ExamView**® Test Generator to create your own chapter test.

FOCUS

❏ Ask volunteers to recall what they had for breakfast that morning and to tell why they chose to eat what they did. Ask for a show of hands to determine how many students tend to eat the same food for breakfast every day. Explain that in this chapter, they will learn how to plan a balanced menu, how to include variety in their meals, how to shop for food, and how to follow recipes.

TEACH

❏ **Reading.** Have students read text pages 421-436.

❏ **Meal Planning.** Have students work in small groups to plan a menu that meets the recommendations of the Food Guide Pyramid. Ask them to make sure that their meals provide a variety of color, size and shape, texture, flavor, and temperature. Have groups share their ideas with the class.

❏ **Explore Food Shopping.** Assign the *Explore* activity on page 426. Allow students to discuss their experiences after they complete the assignment.

❏ **Comparing Brands.** Hold a taste testing comparison of a national brand, a store brand, and a generic brand of the same food item. Items that might be used include corn chips, dry cereal, peanut butter, or canned fruit. Items for tasting should be placed in dishes marked A, B, and C so that students cannot identify brands. Ask students to taste samples and rate each food for appearance, color, texture, and flavor. Ask which samples they prefer and why. Reveal brands following the taste test.

(Continued on next page)

Chapter 23 Lesson Plan continued

❏ **A Closer Look at Food Labels.** Discuss pages 428-429. Ask students to share their reactions to the information provided.

❏ **How to Store Food.** Assign the *How To* activity on page 430, then review the correct storage methods so that students can correct any errors on their charts.

❏ **Food Grades.** Discuss with students the grade labeling system used for poultry and meat. Ask students to describe when they would want to choose the top grade of product available.

ASSESS

❏ Use the reproducible Chapter 23 Test on page 147 of this *Teacher Resource Guide*, or construct your own test using the **Exam***View®* Test Generator found on the *Effective Instruction CD-ROM*.

CLOSE

❏ **Chapter 23 Review & Activities.** Have students answer the questions on text page 437.

❏ Have students write a paragraph explaining important points involved in planning and preparing healthful meals.

Cooking Basics

CHAPTER 24 OBJECTIVES

Students will discover…

◆ how to prepare convenience foods.
◆ the best measuring tool for each task.
◆ techniques for measuring dry and liquid ingredients.
◆ how to cook fruits, vegetables, breads, milk products, meat, poultry, fish, legumes, and eggs.

CHAPTER 24 RESOURCES

STUDENT WORKBOOK
❏ Worksheet #127 through #134

STUDENT MOTIVATION KIT
Project & Activity Cards
❏ #49: Layered Dip

Foods Labs
❏ Lab #4, 5, 6, 7, 9, 10, 11, 15, 16, 17, 19, 21, 22, 24 & 26

Career Investigation Activities
❏ Career Activity #77, 79, 80 & 82

Reteaching Activities
❏ Start Cooking

Enrichment Activities
❏ Using Math in the Kitchen
❏ Cooking Knowledge Quiz
❏ International Cheeses

TEACHER RESOURCE GUIDE
❏ Chapter 24 Test, pp. 149-150

EFFECTIVE INSTRUCTION CD
❏ Use the Word® file to tailor your own Lesson Plan.
❏ Use the **ExamView**® Test Generator to create your own chapter test.

FOCUS

❏ Ask volunteers to describe a cooking disaster they have experienced. Point out that most disasters result from not knowing how to cook a particular kind of food. Explain that in this chapter they will learn the basics of cooking foods from all five of the food groups.

TEACH

❏ **Reading.** Have students read text pages 439-460.

❏ **Explore Measuring Basics.** Assign the *Explore* activity on page 443. Check to make sure students measure the ingredients correctly.

❏ **Seasonal Fruits & Vegetables.** Have students create a brochure showing the months of the year and when seasonal fruits and vegetables are available locally. Ask students to bring in pictures of seasonal fruits and vegetables from magazines to use in the brochure.

❏ **How to Cook a Casserole.** Assign the *How To* activity on page 447.

❏ **Bread Ingredients.** Bring in several labels of bread products. Have students compare the labels to determine the main ingredients. Remind students that labels on food products must list the ingredients in descending order of weight. Ask them how knowing this can help them choose the most nutritious bread products.

(Continued on next page)

Chapter 24 Lesson Plan *continued*

❏ **Pot Sizes.** Display several sizes of pots and pans. Have students estimate the size of pot or pan needed to cook different amounts of breakfast cereal, rice, and pasta. If possible, cook some of the grains to see if students' estimates were correct.

❏ **Taste Test.** Conduct a cheese-tasting lab to introduce students to kinds of cheeses they may not have tasted before. Have them describe flavors. Discuss uses for each type of cheese.

❏ **A Closer Look at Herbs & Spices.** Discuss pages 458-459. Ask students to share their reactions to the information provided.

ASSESS

❏ Use the reproducible Chapter 24 Test on page 149 of this *Teacher Resource Guide*, or construct your own test using the **Exam***View*® Test Generator found on the *Effective Instruction CD-ROM*.

CLOSE

❏ **Chapter 24 Review & Activities.** Have students answer the questions on text page 461.

❏ Ask students to write down the five most interesting facts they learned from reading this chapter.

Chapter 25 Lesson Plan

Microwave Basics

CHAPTER 25 OBJECTIVES

Students will discover…
- how a microwave oven works.
- how to use a microwave oven.
- ways to prepare foods for microwave cooking.
- safety tips for using a microwave oven.

CHAPTER 25 RESOURCES

STUDENT WORKBOOK
- Worksheet #135 through #138

STUDENT MOTIVATION KIT
Project & Activity Cards
- #50: Sweet Popcorn

Foods Labs
- Lab #3, 23 & 24

Career Investigation Activities
- Career Activity #65 & 69

Reteaching Activities
- Microwave Cooking Process
- Microwave Cooking Variables

Enrichment Activities
- Crispy Critters

TEACHER RESOURCE GUIDE
- Chapter 25 Test, pp. 151-152

EFFECTIVE INSTRUCTION CD
- Use the Word® file to tailor your own Lesson Plan.
- Use the **ExamView**® Test Generator to create your own chapter test.

FOCUS

- Ask students to write down ways they use a microwave oven. Make four columns on the board with the following headings: *Cooking, Reheating, Defrosting, Other.* Have students read their responses and write them in the appropriate column on the board. Explain that in this chapter they will learn more about microwave cooking.

TEACH

- **Reading.** Have students read text pages 463-476.
- **Using Potholders.** Point out that potholders should always be used when taking containers out of microwave ovens. It is true that microwaves pass right through containers and into food, leaving the containers cool. Once the food is hot, however, heat is transferred to the container.
- **Microwave Cookware.** Display several pieces of common microwave cookware. Point out to students that items such as these are suitable for microwave use, so it is not always necessary to buy special equipment.
- **A Closer Look at Microwave Cookware.** Discuss pages 468-469. Ask students to share their reactions to the information provided.
- **Explore Microwaving Eggs.** After students have completed the *Explore* activity on page 471 allow time to discuss their evaluations of the scrambled eggs.

(Continued on next page)

Chapter 25 Lesson Plan *continued*

❏ **Microwave Pros and Cons.** Ask students which foods are best suited to microwave cooking. Which are less satisfactory when cooked in a microwave oven? Discuss the advantages and disadvantages of cooking various foods in a microwave oven.

❏ **How to Convert Conventional Oven Recipes.** Assign the *How To* activity on page 475. Invite volunteers to describe the recipe they chose and give their evaluation of the microwave conversion.

ASSESS

❏ Use the reproducible Chapter 25 Test on page 151 of this *Teacher Resource Guide,* or construct your own test using the **Exam** *View*® Test Generator found on the *Effective Instruction CD-ROM.*

CLOSE

❏ **Chapter 25 Review & Activities.** Have students answer the questions on text page 477.

❏ Have students describe something new they learned about microwave cooking by studying this chapter.

Answer Key

CHAPTER 1 REVIEW & ACTIVITIES

Words You Learned

1. *Heredity* is the passing on of traits from parents to their children.
2. *Culture* refers to the ways of thinking, acting, dressing, and speaking shared by a group of people.
3. *Self-concept* is a mental picture of yourself.
4. *Self-esteem* is the ability to respect oneself. Low self-esteem can be caused by dwelling on mistakes, being unrealistic about goals, thinking you must do everything well, and taking criticism personally.
5. *Constructive criticism* is someone's evaluation of a person that helps that person grow and improve.
6. *Initiative* is taking action without being asked.
7. *Values* are one's ideas about right and wrong and about what is important in life.
8. *Self-actualization* means a person realizes his or her full potential.
9. To *prioritize* is to rank in order of importance.
10. *Adolescence* is the period of great growth and change between childhood and adulthood. During adolescence you will be adjusting to many physical and emotional changes.

Check Your Facts

1. Personality is expressed in the way teens look, the way teens communicate, and the way they act.
2. Teens may not feel as good about themselves when something does not work out as they planned. Their self-concept will suffer if they constantly feel bad about themselves.

3. A need is something necessary in order to live. A want is something that you would like to have, but is not necessary for survival.
4. When teens emotions are constantly changing, it may seem as if they lack control over their life.
5. Skin, hair, hands, nails, feet, teeth, and clothing.

Apply Your Learning

1. *Answers will vary.*
2. *Answers will vary.*
3. *Answers will vary but may include:* You will have to decide which value is more important—completing your math homework or being with your friends.
4. *Any three of the following:* admit how you feel and why you feel that way; talk about your feelings with a family member, friend, teacher, or counselor; write down your feelings in a journal; work off your feelings by doing something physical, such as pounding a pillow or taking a walk; if you are angry with another person, wait until you have cooled off before speaking to him or her. Tell the person how you feel and what you need or want.

Words You Learned

1. *Traditions* are customs and beliefs handed down from one generation to another.
2. *Siblings* are brothers and sisters.
3. *Empathy* is the ability of one person to put his or herself in another person's place.
4. Acting *responsibly* means being reliable. For example, you might do your chores without being asked or call home if you are going to be late.

Check Your Facts

1. *Any of the following five:* provide food, clothing, and a place to live; create a loving environment; encourage independence; teach values and life skills; give friendship, guidance, and support.
2. Family relationships are strengthened by becoming involved in each other's daily lives and participating in similar activities, hobbies, and interests.
3. Being responsible and considerate to family members now helps with future relationships because teens will already have practice getting along.
4. Avoid teasing them, speak kindly, and compliment them; share your belongings with them, and ask permission before you use or borrow their belongings; do your share of the chores.
5. *Answers will vary but may include:* by doing the chores that are expected without complaining; following rules and showing respect for other people's feelings; calling home to let someone know you are going to be late; cleaning up after yourself.
6. *Answers will vary but may include:* son, daughter, brother, sister, step-child, grandchild.
7. *Any three of the following:* divorce, remarriage, new siblings, disabilities, job loss, serious illness, death.

Apply Your Learning

1. Support one another through consideration; cooperation; reliability; and understanding.
2. When sharing space, remember to: respect other people's privacy; be considerate of others; and cooperate with family members.
3. Adjust to change by planning ahead; talking about the changes; looking for the positive; and being supportive.

Words You Learned

1. An *acquaintance* is a person you greet or meet fairly often but with whom you do not have a close relationship.
2. *Peers* are people who are the same age.
3. *Expectations* are a person's ideas of what should be or should happen.
4. *Positive peer pressure* can come from a peer group offering a sense of belonging and encouraging positive behavior. *Negative peer pressure* is feeling pushed to participate in activities that go against your values.
5. *Addiction* is a person's physical or mental need for a drug or other substance.
6. *Abstinence* is the only sure way to protect yourself because you don't know the outcome of a potentially dangerous consequence. By saying "no" to behaviors that go against personal values, you will feel better about yourself and have more self-respect.
7. *Assertive* means standing up for yourself in firm but positive ways. For example, saying "no" to drugs.

Check Your Facts

1. An acquaintance is a person you greet or meet fairly often but with whom you do not have a close relationship. A friend is a person who shares similar interests and goals and who can talk to one another.
2. Sharing good times; demonstrating a feeling of acceptance; depending on each other to listen when one person needs to talk about a problem; offering help when it is needed.
3. Caring, sharing, and good communication.
4. *Answers will vary but may include:* Friends may move away or transfer to different schools. Friends may have new responsibilities after school. New interests and activities are discovered.
5. Think ahead, practice refusal skills, suggest other activities, choose your friends carefully, talk to parents and counselors.
6. *Any two of the following:* cigarettes, alcohol, other drugs, inhalants.
7. *Any three of the following:* This goes against my values; I don't want to get hooked on alcohol or drugs; I don't smoke; I value my life too much to do that; I am not into that —go away; I'm not ready; I want to wait until I'm married; I don't want to get AIDS or an STD.
8. *Answers will vary but may include:* Tell parents, a teacher, counselor, or another trusted adult about bullying behavior; do not get angry and strike back; respond firmly or walk away; stick up for another person who is being bullied; stay away from bullies and the places they hang out.

Apply Your Learning

1. You will be liked and accepted more for your individual qualities than for what you do or wear to impress others, and it will improve others.
2. *Answers will vary.*
3. *Answers will vary.*

Words You Learned

1. *Communication* is the process of sending and receiving messages about ideas, feelings, and information.
2. *Body language* is gestures and body movements. Sometimes body language is a substitute for words.
3. How well you listen affects your *perception* of others. Taking time to listen and interpret verbal and nonverbal messages will give you the best information.
4. *Feedback* is important to make sure the listener understood the message.
5. *Gossip* can destroy friendships and ruin reputations. Gossip can also lead to confrontations.
6. *Conflict* can be caused by misunderstandings, differing opinions, gossip and teasing, jealousy or prejudice.
7. *Prejudice* is an opinion about people that is formed without facts or knowledge about those people.
8. *Compromise* is important in resolving a conflict. Each person gives up something in order to reach a solution that satisfies everyone.
9. *Negotiation* is the process of talking about a conflict and deciding how to reach a compromise.
10. *Peer mediation* is a process by which peers help other students find a solution to a conflict before it becomes more serious.

Check Your Facts

1. Body language, personal space, physical appearance.
2. *Answers will vary.*
3. *Compromise* is an agreement in which each person gives up something in order to reach a solution that satisfies everyone. *Negotiation* is the process of talking about a conflict and deciding how to reach a compromise.
4. Open communication lines; state viewpoint; listen carefully; watch body language.

Apply Your Learning

1. When you listen, you try to understand the message that is being communicated.
2. *Answers will vary.*
3. *Answers will vary.*

Words You Learned

1. A *volunteer* is a person who donates time and energy, without pay, to help others. Employees are paid for specified duties.
2. A *citizen* is a member of a community such as a city, state, or country.
3. *Citizenship* is the way you handle your responsibilities as a citizen.
4. *Leadership* is the direction, or guidance, that helps a group accomplish its goals.
5. The ability to guide and motivate others makes a person a good *leader*.
6. *Teamwork* is shown when everyone on the basketball team works together to reach the goal of helping one teammate make a basket during a game.
7. An *apathetic* person is someone who lacks interest.

Check Your Facts

1. *Answers will vary but may include:* Volunteering makes one feel good about oneself. Volunteers gain valuable experiences and a sense of accomplishment.
2. *Answers will vary but may include:* taking a moment to pick up litter and put it in the proper place; returning lost items to the lost-and-found department or to the rightful owner; caring for pets when neighbors go out of town.
3. Motivate others by setting a good example; encourage others with positive words; know when to share responsibilities; have a positive attitude about every task; get all of the facts before making a decision.
4. With the cooperation and support of all members, a team can operate effectively.
5. *Any three of the following:* be respectful of others; be tolerant of different opinions and ideas; be considerate of other people's feelings; don't say everything that is on one's mind, even when one thinks one is right; take every opportunity to compliment others; don't let an apathetic person distract from the task.
6. At home.

Apply Your Learning

1. *Answers will vary.*
2. *Answers will vary but may include:* Obey the law; contribute to the community.
3. *Answers will vary.*

Words You Learned

1. *Goals* are something you want to achieve.
2. Make small goals to help you reach a *long-term goal*. For example, entering a biology project in the science fair in order to become a doctor later on.
3. *Answers will vary.* Must reflect that a *short-term goal* can be reached quickly.
4. A *trade-off* is something that you give up in order to get something more important. For example, if being on the debate team is very important to you, you may need to put off trying out for the band.
5. *Answers will vary.*
6. *Alternatives* are choices.
7. *Consequences* are the results of a choice.

Check Your Facts

1. A realistic goal is one that you can reach. If they are too easy, you may lose interest in them. Realistic goals are both reachable and challenging.
2. Short-term goals can make up smaller steps to reaching a long-term goal.
3. Setting priorities allows you to concentrate on the goals that are most important to you, such as when two or more goals are in conflict with each other. For example, you might want to participate on both cross-country and speech teams, but they meet at the same time so you will have to pick one.
4. *Answers will vary.*
5. A person lets someone else, or the circumstances, make the decision for him or her.
6. *Any four of the following:* Make decisions at the right time; consider the consequences; be willing to take risks; seek advice when needed; accept responsibility for decisions.

Apply Your Learning

1. *Decision-making steps:* (1) Identify the decision to be made or the problem to be solved; (2) List all the possible alternatives; (3) Choose the best alternative; (4) Act on the decision; (5) Evaluate the decision.
2. *Answers will vary.*

Discovering Life Skills • Teacher Resource Guide
Copyright © Glencoe/McGraw-Hill

Words You Learned

1. *Aptitudes* are natural abilities or talents.
2. *Networking* is a great way to research a career because when you seek job information from people you know, you have a good chance of going into the job application process informed and confident. Networking is the most direct way of finding a job.
3. You might want to become an *entrepreneur* because you are your own boss.

Check Your Facts

1. Aptitude tests may give you an incomplete picture of career options because they may not take into consideration your interests.
2. Networking is the most direct way to find a job.
3. Organizations such as FCCLA can help you choose a career because they provide opportunities to participate in events of interest and FCCLA can be a good networking source.
4. The Internet can help you research careers when you: Search *The Occupational Outlook Handbook* or the *Dictionary of Occupational Titles*; read job postings and job descriptions; post a résumé; check out professional organizations; register with on-line employment agencies.
5. You can find resources about education and training beyond high school by talking to your school counselor.
6. Part-time work can help you prepare for full-time employment when you: Learn to get along with your supervisors and coworkers; find out how you like a certain type of work; gain work experience that will be helpful when you apply for a full-time job; become aware of job requirements and other qualities that you need to acquire for full-time work.
7. Technology is a resource that assists you in performing your job duties.

Apply Your Learning

1. *Answers may include any of the following:* Values and goals; abilities and talents; salary.
2. *May include any three of the following:* Education and training needed; job responsibilities; working conditions; salary potential; promotion opportunities; job outlook.
3. *Answers will vary.*

CHAPTER 8 REVIEW & ACTIVITIES

Words You Learned

1. *Comprehension* is understanding what you read.
2. *References* are people who can tell an employer about your character and quality of work.
3. *Flexibility* is important at work because conditions on the job often change.
4. A *team* is a group of people performing work toward a common goal.
5. *Work ethic* is a personal commitment to doing your very best.
6. A *work record* is a written record of how well an employee performs on the job.
7. A *promotion* is a move into a job with more responsibility.
8. To *terminate* employment means to leave the job.

Check Your Facts

1. Develop basic knowledge and skills because they serve as tools to help you function in life and at work. For example, you will need reading and writing skills to fill out a job application and to create a résumé. To understand the information on your paycheck and to budget your money, you will need math skills.
2. The document you must complete in order to get a job is called a job application.
3. The purpose of a job interview is to meet with an employer and discuss your qualifications. It also gives you a chance to learn more about the job. It is an opportunity to ask questions about the job.
4. Demonstrate responsibility as an employee by: knowing your job responsibilities.
5. Teamwork is an important employability skill to possess because the better your relationships are with your employer, supervisor, and coworkers, and perhaps customers or clients, the more you will enjoy work and experience success.
6. A promotion means to move into a job with more responsibility and possibly more money.
7. Terminate employment by giving notice soon enough for your employer to find a replacement by the time you leave the job. A two-week notice is considered minimum; giving a letter of resignation. The letter should be given to your immediate supervisor. The letter should state the exact date you expect to be your last day of employment. It should also thank the employer for his or her help during your time with the company. Be sure to give a brief explanation of why you are leaving.

Apply Your Learning

1. *Answers will vary but may include:* Where and when will I work and what will my job duties be?
2. Accept the offer; ask for time to consider the offer; turn down the job offer.
3. *Answers will vary, but may include:* A personal commitment to doing your very best; being responsible; working well on a team; being flexible; being reliable.

Words You Learned

1. *Parenthood* is important because parents are responsible for providing a safe, loving, and stimulating environment for their children.
2. Another word for *guidance* is direction.
3. *Discipline* is the task of teaching a child which behavior is acceptable and which is not.
4. *Child abuse* means physical, emotional, or sexual injury to children.
5. *Child neglect* is failure to meet a child's physical and emotional needs.
6. *Developmental tasks* are achievements, such as walking and talking that can be expected at various ages and stages of growth.
7. *Attention span* refers to the length of time a person can concentrate on any one thing.
8. *Independent play* means playing alone and showing little interest in interacting with other children.
9. Preschoolers are ready to engage in *cooperative play*—playing together with one or two other children and sharing toys.

Check Your Facts

1. *Any three of the following:* mother, father, grandmother, grandfather, or another adult.
2. Fulfill a child's emotional and social needs by holding, cuddling, comforting, kissing, hugging and patting him or her.
3. It is important to be consistent with children, which means reacting the same way to a situation each time it occurs. It also means that you follow through and do what you say you will do. For example, if you say that you will take away a toy the next time a child throws it, you should do so. When you are consistent, children know what to expect.
4. Children learn from exploring their environment with their five senses—sight, hearing, taste, touch, and smell.
5. Play benefits preschoolers by teaching them to: take turns, share with others, and learn how to get along in a group.

Apply Your Learning

1. *Independent play*—playing alone and showing little interest in interacting with other children. *Cooperative play*—engaging with several children.
2. *Answers will vary but may include: Infants*—crib mobiles, rattles, stuffed toys, clutch balls, nesting toys, stacking toys, cloth ball, blocks. *Toddlers*—take-apart toys, push-pull toys, riding toys, balls, dolls, crayons, books, large blocks, sand box. *Preschoolers*—modeling clay, finger paint, educational card games, books, puppets, puzzles.

Words You Learned

1. Families *childproof* their homes to make a safe environment for their children.
2. Babysitters can protect against *intruders* by: making sure that all doors and windows are locked; not opening the door for any stranger; calling a neighbor, another trusted adult, or dialing 9-1-1 if a stranger does not go away.
3. To *redirect* a child means you turn his or her attention to something else, such as a game, toy or puzzle.

Check Your Facts

1. If a child swallows poison, call the poison control center.
2. The questions you should ask before you accept a babysitting job are: The number and ages of the children you will be watching; the time you will need to arrive; how long the parents plan to be gone; the rate of pay you will receive.
3. You can learn the children's family rules by asking the parents to go over them in front of the children.
4. Babies communicate their needs by crying.

Apply Your Learning

1. Call 9-1-1.
2. All poisonous items should be kept in locked cabinets. Or kept on a high shelf, out of children's reach.
3. A reliable babysitter keeps a constant, careful eye on the children; keeps an accurate list of telephone messages; leaves the house as neat as it was upon arrival; doesn't allow friends to visit; doesn't open door to strangers.

Words You Learned

1. People are *consumers* when they buy goods and services. At some point everyone buys goods and services.
2. An *advertisement* is a message that persuades consumers to buy a product or service.
3. *Comparison shopping*, or checking quality and price and reading labels and guarantees, will help you get the best value for your money.
4. A *warranty* is the manufacturer's written promise to repair or replace a product if it does not work as claimed.
5. *Shoplifting*, or taking items from a store without paying for them, is a crime because it is stealing.
6. Action taken to correct a wrong is called *redress*. Consumers can seek redress if they have a problem with a product.
7. *Income* is the amount of money you earn or receive regularly.
8. *Expenses* are the monies you spend to buy goods and services.
9. A *budget* is a plan for using your money.
10. *Credit* is not free. Interest on the unpaid balance is the charge for the use of credit.

Check Your Facts

1. The choices you have as a consumer are what to buy, where to buy it, and when to buy it.
2. The three factors that influence your buying decisions are: peers, habit, and advertising.
3. Three ways to get product information before you go to a store are: to talk to family and friends; read consumer magazines; and check advertisements.
4. When selecting a store consider the item you want to buy, the price you are willing to pay, and the service you need.
5. Shoplifting affects the price you pay for goods because it costs businesses millions of dollars each year in lost goods. These losses are passed on to consumers as increased prices.
6. The purpose of keeping an expense record is to help improve your spending habits.
7. You should have a savings plan to help you save for unexpected events and for the future.

Apply Your Learning

1. *Answers will vary.*
2. Items on sale may be less expensive than regular-priced items, but may not be of the same quality. Look carefully at products on sale to see if they are, in fact, bargains. Higher-priced items may be of good quality, but they may also contain features that you don't need.
3. *Any four of the following:* Cash, layaway plan, check, debit cards, credit cards.

CHAPTER 12 REVIEW & ACTIVITIES

Words You Learned

1. The purpose of *management* is using what you have to accomplish something, being organized and planning ahead.
2. A *resource* is helpful because the information or expertise can be used to help you meet your goals.
3. To *prioritize* means to rank tasks in order of importance.
4. You waste time when you *procrastinate* because you think and worry about the task you need to complete rather than just completing it.
5. *Stress* is the body's reaction to changes around it.

Check Your Facts

1. The three types of resources are: personal resources, material resources, and community resources.
2. To prioritize tasks is to rank the tasks in order of importance.
3. The benefits of good time management are that you will have more time for special activities, such as playing basketball or starting a stamp collection; you won't constantly be late or forget to do important tasks; you will have more time for yourself and others.
4. Three time-management tools are: using a calendar; using a list; making a time schedule.
5. *Any four of the following:* divide big jobs into small tasks; do two tasks at the same time; avoid interruptions; stick with a task until it is done; establish routines for daily tasks.
6. Stress can motivate you because it can help you accomplish your goals in life. For example, the stress of wanting to make the soccer team would motivate you to exercise and practice.

Apply Your Learning

1. Time, energy, knowledge, skills, and people.
2. *Answers will vary.*
3. *Answers will vary.*

Words You Learned

1. A *floor plan* is a drawing of a room and how its furniture is arranged. It allows you to see how furniture fits together without physically moving furniture.
2. The *traffic pattern* is the path people take to move around and enter and exit the room.
3. *Design* is the art of combining elements in a pleasing way.
4. *Accessories* are interesting items added to make a space more personal.

Check Your Facts

1. A floor plan can help you organize space because it allows you to see how furniture fits together without physically moving furniture.
2. Warm colors are: red, yellow, and orange.
3. Cool colors are: blue, green, and violet.
4. The six principles of design are: balance, emphasis, unity, scale, rhythm, and proportion.
5. The five reasons to keep your home clean and neat are: It saves time and energy; clothes and other possessions last longer; family members stay healthier in a clean home; most home accidents can be prevented; security measures can keep a home safe.

6. *Any two of the following:* If something is spilled on the floor, wipe it up immediately; place nonskid pads under small rugs so that they don't slide; be sure to use nonskid strips or mats in bathtubs and showers; make sure that stairs are in good repair, well lit, and free from clutter. Stairs should also have handrails.

Apply Your Learning

1. *Answers will vary but may include:* By hanging up clothes or putting them in the hamper; returning personal grooming items to their proper place.
2. *Answers will vary but may include:* Organizing rooms for more than one function to make the best use of space, equipment, and furniture.
3. *Answers will vary but may include:* Use white or light colors on the walls to make a room look larger.

Words You Learned

1. *Natural resources* are materials that are supplied by nature. These include air, water, soil, and the energy derived from coal, oil, and gas.
2. Causes of *pollution* include any three of the following: burning of fuels; burning leaves or trash; chemicals, including those that kill insects and those used as cooling agents; human wastes, detergents, and the chemicals used to kill insects or to fertilize crops.
3. Everyone needs to practice *conservation* in order to save our resources.
4. *Landfills* are huge pits where waste is buried between layers of earth.
5. *Decompose* means to break down. For example, waste is buried and it breaks down to become part of the soil.
6. *Incineration* means disposing of waste by burning.
7. *Biodegradable* products are those that break down and are absorbed by the environment.
8. *Recycling* is turning waste items into products that can be used.

Check Your Facts

1. *Any 10 of the following:* Turn off lights when you are not using them; use hot water sparingly; keep doors to unused rooms closed; use the microwave oven; cook several items at the same time and avoid opening the oven door while foods are cooking; run the dishwasher only with a full load; avoid leaving the refrigerator door open; turn the thermostat up during the summer; keep the thermostat down to 68°F in the winter; use lined drapes; seal cracks around doors and windows.
2. The major causes of air pollution include: the release of poisonous gases such as car exhaust fumes; smoke from sources such as fireplaces, barbecues, and burning leaves; chemicals, including those that kill insects and those used as cooling agents in air conditioners and refrigerators.
3. An energy-efficient appliance requires less energy and will reduce pollution in the environment.
4. Biodegradable products help the environment by returning to soil, rather than filling landfills.
5. *Practice outdoor safety by doing any of the following:* Wear the right clothing for the weather; use marked trails and designated campsites; tell someone where you are going and when you expect to return; avoid being out in extreme temperatures and electrical storms; know how much you are really capable of doing; use the correct equipment for each activity; know the safety rules and follow them; remember to warm up before and cool down after an activity to avoid injury; use the buddy system; use sunscreen to protect your skin from ultraviolet rays.

Apply Your Learning

1. *Answers will vary but may include:* Use air, water, land, and energy wisely; make an effort to be energy-efficient at home; be a concerned citizen who cares about the environment and works with others to keep it clean; reduce the amount of paper you throw away, using only washable cups and plates, and using cloth napkins; avoid buying disposable products; pre-cycle, or avoid buying products that use more packaging than necessary; plan meals carefully so there is little waste of food and energy for cooking; use cloth grocery bags instead of paper or plastic ones; buy products that are biodegradable, or broken down and absorbed by the environment; reuse items rather than throwing them away.
2. *Answers will vary.*

Words You Learned

1. Some people wear designer labels, logos, and other recognized names and symbols to show their *status*.
2. *Style* is the design of a garment.
3. *Fashions* are styles of clothing that are popular at a particular time.
4. *Fads* are very popular for a short time.
5. *Classic styles* remain in fashion for a long time and will save you money because you will have them for many years.
6. The three basic *hues* are red, yellow, and blue.
7. A light value of a hue is called a *tint*.
8. A dark value of a hue is called a *shade*.
9. Color *intensity* is the brightness or dullness of a color.
10. You can use *texture* to change the way you look. For example, dull textures make you look smaller. Nubby or shiny textures add bulk.

Check Your Facts

1. It's best not to spend a lot of money on fad clothing because it quickly goes out of style.
2. The three main directions of lines in fashions are: Vertical lines, which make you look taller and thinner; horizontal lines, which make you look shorter and wider; and diagonal lines, which make you look taller and thinner or shorter and wider, depending on the length and angle of the lines.
3. Garment shape affects the way you look depending on the lines. For example, straight-leg, tapered, and flared pants can all look different on the same body.
4. Texture is created by using different yarns and weaves in making fabric.
5. Use accessories to draw attention to your best features and away from less attractive ones. For instance, a wide belt can emphasize a slim waistline. A watchband or bracelet can draw attention to graceful hands.

Apply Your Learning

1. *Answers will vary.*
2. *Answers will vary.*
3. *Answers will vary.*

Words You Learned

1. *Fibers* are the tiny strands that make up fabric.
2. *Woven fabrics* are made on a loom by interlacing lengthwise and crosswise threads at right angles.
3. *Knit fabrics* are fabrics made by looping threads together.
4. *Grain* is the direction the threads run in a fabric. Well-constructed clothes are cut on grain, with the threads running straight up and down and straight across.
5. A *shopping plan* is a strategy for spending the money you have available to purchase the clothing you need or want.

Check Your Facts

1. The four natural fibers are: cotton, linen, silk, and wool. Sources for each are as follows: Cotton comes from the seedpod of the cotton plant; linen comes from the flax plant; silk comes from silkworms; wool comes from the hair of sheep.
2. Synthetic fibers are made partially or entirely from chemicals. For example, polyester and nylon are two types of synthetic fibers.
3. If the fabric is off grain, the garment will appear to sag to one side after a few washings.

4. *Answers will vary but may include:* Start with two or three basic outfits; make the best use of what you have; take good care of your clothes; compare cost and quality; take advantage of sales; learn to sew.
5. Pre-treat a stain by applying a stain remover before laundering.

Apply Your Learning

1. *Answers will vary but may include:* Consider clothing budget; quality of fabric and construction; number of times item will be worn.
2. The style of a garment might be loose or close fitting, but it should still fit properly.
3. *Answers will vary.*

Making Connections—Get Involved!

Wear the garment 80 times.

Add the cost of the garment and the cost of cleaning it: *(Note: the garment is worn twice between cleanings, which changes the $12 cleaning amount to $6 per wear)*

$50 + $6 = $56

Divide the total cost by the number of times you will wear the garment:

$56 ÷ 80 = .7¢

Estimated cost per wearing = .70¢

Words You Learned

1. A sewing *pattern* is a plan for making a garment or project. It contains paper shapes of the various pieces and gives the instructions for sewing.
2. *Darts* are used to give shape to a garment.
3. Hemming pants to make them shorter is an *alteration* that could make a garment fit better.
4. Fabrics with *nap*, contain a one-way texture.
5. Basic *notions* include: thread; fasteners such as zippers, buttons, snaps, hook and loop tape; elastic; interfacing.

Check Your Facts

1. *Answers will vary depending upon the brand of sewing machine; refer to the user's manual.*
2. *Regular stitch*—a medium-length stitch used for sewing most projects; *basting stitch*—a very long stitch used for holding layers of fabric together temporarily; *reinforcement stitch*—a short stitch used to strengthen a corner or a point; *zigzag stitch*—a sideways stitch used to make buttonholes, finish seam edges, and sew special seams.
3. Check the sewing machine manual for instructions on controlling the speed on a sewing machine.
4. *The back of the pattern envelope contains any three of the following:* A drawing showing the pattern pieces and construction features, such as darts; a chart that tells you how much fabric to buy for the style and size pattern you are using; recommendations on the types of fabrics that can be used; additional materials you will need, such as thread and buttons.
5. *Look for any of the following to help you choose an easy-to-make pattern:* Patterns marked "easy;" number of pattern pieces; number of seams; garment fit, such as those with loose-fitting styles; simple closures, such as elastic waists, snaps, and hooks.

Apply Your Learning

1. *Answers will vary.*
2. Most important measurements for blouses and tops are the bust measurement; for shirts, the chest and neck measurements; for full skirts, the waist measurement; for pants and semi-fitted skirts, the hip measurement.

Making Connections—Get Involved!

Add materials costs to the entry fee. *(Note there are two entry fees):*

$75 + $10 + $10 = $95

Divide the total by 10 dolls.

$95 \div 10 = $9.50

Multiply the number of hours it takes to complete a doll by the amount charged per hour.

$3 \times $15 = $45

Add this total to $9.50 to determine the amount Caitlin should charge per doll.

$45 + $9.50 = $54.00

Caitlin should charge $54.00 per doll.

Words You Learned

1. *Selvage* is the tightly woven edge of the fabric that has no visible loose threads.
2. A garment cut on the *bias* is cut on the diagonal.
3. From a pattern *guide sheet* you can learn general information on how to use the pattern, see a diagram of the pattern pieces, and read an explanation of the pattern markings, and layouts.
4. The purpose of *layouts* is to see how the pattern pieces should be placed on the fabric.
5. Pattern *markings* are guides on the pattern pieces. Markings tell you where darts, dots, fold lines, and buttonholes are located, making it easier to lay out, cut, and sew with patterns.
6. *Ease* is the amount of fullness added for movement and comfort.
7. *Staystitching* prevents stretching and helps in turning under edges of hems and bands.
8. *Casings* are used if your garment has a pull-on waistband or sleeve band. They are fabric tunnels made to enclose elastic or drawstrings.
9. The name of the large cylinders used to hold serging thread are called *cones*.
10. *Loopers* are the rounded parts that hold the thread inside a serger.

Check Your Facts

1. Preshrink fabric so that after you sew the garment it does not shrink the first time you clean it.
2. *Reduce bulk in seams using any two of the following:* Trimming the seam allowance to ⅜ or ¼ inch; grading by trimming seam allowances to different widths; clipping by cutting slits into the trimmed seam allowance every ¼ to ½ inch; or notching by cutting little Vs or triangles in the seam allowance.
3. Two types of seam finishes are pinking or zigzagging.
4. A serger cannot sew a single line of locked stitches, whereas a sewing machine can. However, a serger allows you to use a greater variety of fabrics, including stretchy knits and sheers. You can use a serger to produce decorative stitching and reversible seams.
5. Chain stitch; flatlock stitch; overedge stitch; overlock stitch; rolled hem stitch; safety stitch.

Apply Your Learning

1. *Prepare the pattern as follows:* Cut apart the pieces you will use, but do not trim them. Put the pattern pieces that you will not use back in the envelope; Study each pattern piece, and refer to the guide sheet to find out what each marking means; If the pattern pieces are wrinkled, press them with a warm, dry iron.
2. Test your marking device on a fabric scrap to make sure the marks come out of the fabric completely.

Words You Learned

1. Art can provide an *outlet* for your emotions.
2. A *gusset* is a triangle- or diamond-shaped piece of fabric cut on the bias that can be added to a garment for a decorative or functional purpose.

Check Your Facts

1. *Answers will vary but may include:* Sewing, painting, writing, crafting.
2. *Answers may include any two of the following:* Paints, dyes, stamps, beads, buttons, trims, cutting, tearing, folding, dyeing.
3. *Answers may include any two of the following:* Paint the walls; use glow-in-the-dark thread to embroider stars and stick them to the ceiling; decorate furniture; decorate lampshades; make toss pillows; decorate picture frames.
4. *Answers will vary.*

Apply Your Learning

1. *Answers will vary.*
2. *Answers will vary.*
3. *Answers will vary.*

CHAPTER 20 REVIEW & ACTIVITIES

Words You Learned

1. *Nutrients* are substances that are important for the body's growth and care.
2. Reaching for your best level of health is called *wellness*.
3. A *calorie* is a unit used to measure the energy used by the body and the energy that food supplies to the body.
4. *Digestion* is the process of breaking down food into a form the body can use.
5. *Proteins* are nutrients that are needed to build, repair, and maintain body cells and tissues.
6. *Amino acids* are the building blocks that make up proteins.
7. *Carbohydrates* are the starches and sugars that give the body most of its energy. Starches are found in grains, such as oats, rice, and wheat.
8. *Fiber* is plant material that your body cannot digest.
9. Your body produces all the *cholesterol* it needs, so you don't need to add it to your diet. In fact, diets high in cholesterol have been linked to an increased risk of heart disease.
10. *Any three of the following vitamins:* vitamin A, B-complex vitamins, thiamine, riboflavin, niacin, vitamin B_6, folic acid, vitamin B_{12}, pantothenic acid, biotin, vitamin C, vitamin D, vitamin E, vitamin K.
11. *Any three of the following minerals:* calcium, fluoride, iodine, iron, magnesium, phosphorous, potassium, sodium, zinc.
12. To prevent *osteoporosis*, absorb plenty of calcium.

Check Your Facts

1. Your diet is the source for energy. A good diet provides more energy.
2. There are six kinds of nutrients: proteins, carbohydrates, fats, vitamins, minerals, and water. There functions are: *Proteins*—help build, repair, and maintain body cells and tissues; *carbohydrates*—provide energy and fiber; *fats*—provide energy and supply essential fatty acids for normal growth and healthy skin; *vitamins*, *minerals*, and *water*—help regulate the work of the body's systems.
3. *Answers will vary but may include:* meat; fish; poultry; milk; cheese; eggs.
4. Teens must get enough calcium in their diet because it is essential for normal bone and tooth development.
5. When you eat food with more calories than your body needs you gain weight.

Apply Your Learning

1. *Answers will vary.*
2. *Answers will vary.*

Words You Learned

1. *Fitness* is the ability to handle daily events in a healthy way.
2. *Stamina* is the ability to focus on a single activity for a long time.
3. *Obesity* is a condition in which a person's weight is 20 percent or more above his or her healthy weight.
4. *Eating disorders* are extreme eating behaviors that can lead to depression, anxiety, and even death. Eating disorders are psychological problems that are related to food.
5. *Anorexia Nervosa* is the eating disorder that involves starving yourself.
6. *Bulimia nervosa* is the eating disorder that involves vomiting or the use of laxatives.
7. *Binge eating* means not being able to stop eating.
8. *Fad diets* are often unbalanced, as they don't provide all of the nutrients you need. Some may even cause physical harm.

Check Your Facts

1. Obese people are at greater risk for such illnesses as diabetes and heart disease.
2. People who are underweight often aren't eating enough or properly. This means that they aren't getting the nutrients they need.
3. In order to control your weight you have to balance the calories you get from the foods you eat with the calories you use for energy.
4. Calories are related to your diet and the amount of exercise you get because you gain weight when you consume more calories than your body uses. You lose weight when your body uses more calories than you consume. To maintain your weight, you must make sure that the calories you eat equal those you burn as energy.
5. A sensible approach to controlling your weight is to combine a good diet with exercise.

Apply Your Learning

1. *Answers will vary.*
2. *Answers will vary.*
3. *Answers will vary.*

CHAPTER 22 REVIEW & ACTIVITIES

Words You Learned

1. In mild cases of food *contamination*, people may experience headaches, stomach cramps, and fever. In some cases, medical attention may be necessary. Severe food poisoning can result in death.
2. You could be infected with *E. coli* by eating hamburger that has not been fully cooked.
3. Avoid *salmonella* poisoning by thoroughly cooking all meat, poultry, fish, and eggs. Wash your hands, knife, and cutting board with soap and hot water whenever you cut raw meat, fish, or poultry.
4. *Perishable* foods include all of the following: meat, poultry, fish, eggs, and dairy products.
5. *Flammable* items include: paper bags, potholders, kitchen towels, curtains, and plastic containers.
6. Electrical appliances, such as forks, knives, or other metal utensils, *conduct* electricity and can cause electrical shock.

Check Your Facts

1. Bacteria causes food poisoning.
2. To keep leftovers from spoiling, refrigerate or freeze them immediately after the meal.
3. Falls, burns, fires, and cuts.
4. *Prevent kitchen falls by:* Standing on a short stepladder or a sturdy step stool with a waist-high hand bar to get at high or hard-to-reach items; turning pot and pan handles toward the center of the stove or counter so that the pots or pans won't get knocked over; cleaning up spilled foods or liquids immediately; keeping cupboard doors and drawers closed when not in use.
5. *Any three of the following:* A paring knife is used for trimming and peeling fruits and vegetables. A chef's knife is used for chopping and mincing. A bread knife has a scalloped edge and is used to cut through breads without tearing them. A carving knife is used to slice meat. A cleaver is used to cut through thick meat and bones.

Apply Your Learning

1. *Answers will vary.*
2. *Answers will vary.*
3. *Answers will vary.*

CHAPTER 23 REVIEW & ACTIVITIES

Words You Learned

1. You might serve an *appetizer* before dinner if dinner is not yet ready or to give people a chance to visit one another.
2. You can choose a combination of foods from the five food groups that fit your *meal patterns*.
3. You add a *garnish* to a dish to decorate the food.
4. *Texture* means the way food feels when it is eaten. For example, raw vegetables are crisp and pudding is smooth.

Check Your Facts

1. Color, size and shape, texture, flavor, and temperature.
2. Skills, equipment, ingredients, money, and time.
3. *Any four of the following:* The name of the food; the name and address of the product's manufacturer; the nutritional content; including serving size, calories, and nutrient amounts per serving; a list of ingredients in order of amount; the total weight.
4. *Boil* means to cook in liquid hot enough to bubble rapidly. *Broil* means to cook under direct heat.

5. *Whip* means to beat fast with an electric mixer, rotary beater, or wire whip to add enough air to make the mixture fluffy. *Blend* means to stir until ingredients are completely mixed.
6. *Tbsp.* = tablespoon; *tsp.* = teaspoon; *ml* = milliliter; *L* = liter.

Apply Your Learning

1. *Answers may vary but should include:* You can choose a combination of foods from the five food groups that fit your meal pattern.
2. Three ways to save money when shopping for groceries are: Clip any coupons; adjust your menus to take advantage of weekly specials; take a calculator with you so you can keep track of what you are spending.
3. Store frozen foods first when unpacking groceries.
4. If you know how to read and follow recipes, you will greatly increase your chances of success in the kitchen.
5. You must choose foods that can be prepared within the time allowed. It is also important to make sure that all foods are ready to serve at the right time. Some dishes take longer than others to prepare, and some foods take longer than others to cook.

Words You Learned

1. *Convenience foods* are already partly prepared to save you time.
2. Milk *scalds* when you bring it slowly to a temperature just below the boiling point.
3. Milk *curdles* when tomatoes or fruit juices are added because they contain acid.
4. *Legumes* are dry beans and peas.
5. Another name for a main-dish pie is *quiche*.
6. An *omelet* is fried before it is topped with ingredients and folded over.

Check Your Facts

1. If ingredients are not measured accurately a baked good, for example, may not rise or it may burn.
2. Three ingredients that could be measured in a liquid measuring cup are milk, water, and oil.
3. Strawberries are an example of a seasonal fruit.
4. To prevent vitamin and mineral loss during cooking: Add as little water as possible; use a lid to speed cooking time; avoid overcooking.
5. Three tips for cooking with cheese are: Use low to medium heat; grate or shred hard cheeses, such as cheddar, before adding them to other ingredients. The cheese will blend faster and more evenly; add cheese to sauces or casseroles at the end of the cooking time so that the cheese won't become overcooked.

Apply Your Learning

1. *Answers will vary.*
2. *Answers will vary.*
3. *Answers will vary.*

Words You Learned

1. Inside a microwave oven, a *magnetron* heats food by vibrating the molecules of water, fat, and sugar inside the food. This creates heat and cooks the food.
2. Avoid *arcing* by not placing metal containers in the microwave oven.
3. *Variables* are conditions that determine how long a food needs to be cooked and at what power level.
4. *Superheating* occurs when a liquid is heated in a container that doesn't allow bubble formation, or boiling. The liquid can explode when it comes into contact with atmospheric pressure. For example, when a spoon breaks the surface, the hot liquid can explode.

Check Your Facts

1. It is important to use microwave-safe containers when cooking food in a microwave oven to avoid fires.
2. Use a microwave oven to defrost food so you can cook it sooner than when defrosting traditionally.
3. *Any three of the following:* paper, plastic, glass, Corningware®, Stoneware®.
4. Standing time is required to let the food temperatures equalize.

5. (A) Use "microwave safe" dishes to avoid fires and other accidents. (B) Remove covers slowly after food is cooked to avoid steam burns. (C) Do not microwave foods in containers that are completely sealed to avoid the container bursting. (D) Do not use an extension cord with a microwave oven or plug it into the same electrical outlet as other large electrical appliances. (E) If the oven door does not close tightly or if you hear unusual sounds coming from the oven do not use it. (F) If there are sparks inside the oven or if there is a fire, turn off the oven or unplug it immediately and get help.

Apply Your Learning

1. They produce microwaves, or energy waves that penetrate food and agitate its molecules, thereby cooking the food faster than a conventional oven.
2. *Answers will vary but may include:* You must use only "microwave safe" dishes; steam can build up and cause burns; when pressure from steam builds, the cooking container can burst; sparks can occur if metal is used in the microwave; superheating can occur when a liquid is heated in a container that doesn't allow bubble formation, or boiling. The result could be severe burns if the superheated liquid comes into contact with your skin.
3. Pressure from the steam inside the egg would cause the eggshell to crack.
4. Fire is the greatest safety risk involved with microwave ovens.

Testing Program

Contents

Discovering Yourself

MATCHING

Directions: Match each definition in the left column with the correct term from the right column. Write the letter of the term in the space provided. Do not use any term more than once. Some terms will not be used.

Definitions

_____ **1.** Taking action without being asked

_____ **2.** Ways of thinking, acting, and speaking shared by a group of people

_____ **3.** The passing on of traits from parents to their children

_____ **4.** The ability to respect yourself and use your own judgment

_____ **5.** To rank in order of importance

_____ **6.** Ideas about right and wrong and what is important

Terms

A. prioritize
B. heredity
C. self-esteem
D. initiative
E. constructive criticism
F. values
G. adolescence
H. culture

FILL IN THE BLANK

Directions: In the space provided, write the word (or words) that BEST completes each sentence.

_____ **7.** By watching __?__ such as parents and teachers, you learn how to act in certain situations. *(2 words)*

_____ **8.** The mental picture you have of yourself is called your __?__.

_____ **9.** Excitement, sadness, and frustration are all examples of __?__.

_____ **10.** During adolescence, you will experience both __?__ and emotional changes.

_____ **11.** __?__ involves taking care of your skin, hair, nails, teeth, hands, feet, and clothing.

(Continued on next page)

Chapter 1 Test *continued*

_____ **12.** Use a __?__ to protect your skin from the sun.

_____ **13.** To avoid dental problems, choose a toothpaste that contains __?__.

MULTIPLE CHOICE

Directions: In the space provided, write the letter of the choice that BEST completes the statement or answers the question.

_____ **14.** You can improve your self-concept by doing all of the following EXCEPT __?__.
    A. help others without being asked   **C.** do what everyone else is doing
    B. take responsibility for your actions   **D.** think carefully before you act

_____ **15.** An effective way to deal with constructive criticism is to __?__.
    A. listen to it, then ignore it   **C.** reject the criticism
    B. accept it and learn from it   **D.** walk away

_____ **16.** All of the following are ways to show responsibility EXCEPT __?__.
    A. cover up your mistakes   **C.** take care of your health
    B. do your best at school   **D.** follow rules at home and at school

_____ **17.** The highest level of achievement in Maslow's hierarchy of human needs is __?__.
    A. self-esteem   **C.** self-importance
    B. self-concept   **D.** self-actualization

_____ **18.** When you prioritize your values, you __?__.
    A. rank them in order of importance
    B. compare values with those of your peers
    C. share them with family members
    D. explain why you chose them

_____ **19.** All of the following are healthy ways to deal with anger EXCEPT __?__.
    A. talk about your feelings with someone you trust
    B. write about your feelings in a private journal
    C. cover up your feelings and pretend everything is fine
    D. calm down and then tell the person how you feel

_____ **20.** To take care of your skin, do all of the following EXCEPT __?__.
    A. avoid picking or squeezing pimples
    B. avoid washing your face with soap
    C. use a sunscreen when you are out in the sun
    D. drink six to eight glasses of water a day

Discovering Life Skills • Teacher Resource Guide
Copyright © Glencoe/McGraw-Hill

Your Family

MATCHING

Directions: Match each definition in the left column with the correct term from the right column. Write the letter of the term in the space provided. Do not use any term more than once.

Definitions

Terms

A. empathy
B. supportive
C. siblings
D. responsible
E. traditions
F. consideration

_____ **1.** brothers and sisters

_____ **2.** customs and beliefs handed down from one generation to another

_____ **3.** respect for other people's feelings

_____ **4.** reliable and respectful

_____ **5.** the ability to put yourself in another person's place

_____ **6.** helpful and reassuring

MULTIPLE CHOICE

Directions: In the space provided, write the letter of the choice that BEST completes the statement or answers the question.

_____ **7.** You can enrich family life by doing all of the following EXCEPT __?__.
  A. share daily events with family members
  B. discuss books and movies
  C. avoid talking about your problems
  D. plan special family celebrations

_____ **8.** When you show empathy to another person, you __?__.
  A. put yourself in the other person's place
  B. explain the best way to solve a problem
  C. ask what is troubling the person
  D. ask the person his or her opinion

(Continued on next page)

Chapter 2 Test continued

_____ 9. All of the following are effective ways of getting along with siblings EXCEPT __?__.
   A. speak kindly and give compliments
   B. tease them only when they deserve it
   C. share your belongings with them
   D. ask their permission before you borrow anything

_____ 10. All of the following are effective ways of sharing space in the home EXCEPT __?__.
   A. respect other people's privacy
   B. put your belongings away
   C. keep your music turned low
   D. let others clean up after you

_____ 11. The stage of the family life cycle when teens become independent and leave home is called the __?__.
   A. beginning stage
   B. launching stage
   C. independence stage
   D. leaving stage

_____ 12. When adjusting to change, do all of the following EXCEPT __?__.
   A. prepare for the change by planning ahead
   B. help family members by being supportive
   C. keep your feelings about the change to yourself
   D. focus on the positive aspects of the change

FILL IN THE BLANK

Directions: In the space provided, write the word (or words) that BEST completes each sentence.

_____ 13. Families have different ways of __?__ themselves and their emotions.

_____ 14. By sharing hobbies and interests, family members __?__ their ties with one another.

_____ 15. You can show empathy by respecting other people's __?__.

_____ 16. You can help your parents understand your feelings by __?__ with them.

_____ 17. Sharing space is easier at busy times if everyone agrees on a __?__.

_____ 18. Knowing how to __?__ to change is necessary in all families.

_____ 19. A change in the __?__ may cause a job loss and result in less money for the family.

_____ 20. One of the most difficult changes for a family to deal with is the __?__ of a family member.

Discovering Life Skills • Teacher Resource Guide
Copyright © Glencoe/McGraw-Hill

Chapter 3 Test

Your Friendships

MATCHING

Directions: Match each definition in the left column with the correct term from the right column. Write the letter of the term in the space provided. Do not use any term more than once.

Definitions

_____ 1. Ideas about what should be or should happen

_____ 2. People the same age as you

_____ 3. The influence you feel to go along with your peers

_____ 4. A person you meet often but who is not a personal friend

_____ 5. A physical or mental need for a drug or other substance

_____ 6. Strategies that enable you to say "no" effectively

_____ 7. Standing up for yourself in a firm but positive way

_____ 8. Refusal to participate in unsafe behaviors or activities

Terms

A. addiction
B. expectations
C. acquaintance
D. peers
E. abstinence
F. peer pressure
G. assertive
H. refusal skills

FILL IN THE BLANK

Directions: In the space provided, write the word (or words) that BEST completes each sentence.

_____ 9. A __?__ is someone who shares similar interests, goals, and values.

_____ 10. Good friendships are based on a(n) __?__-and-__?__ relationship.

_____ 11. A good friend helps by __?__ when you need to talk about a problem.

_____ 12. Caring, sharing, and good communication help to __?__ friendships.

_____ 13. In order to keep friends, you have to be willing to __?__ something.

(Continued on next page)

Chapter 3 Test continued

_____ **14.** Acceptance by peers strengthens your __?__.

_____ **15.** Some changes in friendships are due to changing __?__ about what should happen.

_____ **16.** When faced with peer pressure, you need to follow your own __?__.

_____ **17.** Refusal skills will help you avoid __?__, such as tobacco and alcohol. *(2 words)*

_____ **18.** Being assertive means standing up for what you believe and speaking in a __?__ manner.

TRUE/FALSE

Directions: Read each statement carefully. If the statement is true, place a plus (+) in the space provided. If the statement is false, replace the italicized word(s) with the correct word(s). Write your answer in the space provided.

_____ **19.** *Casual friends* are people you know very well and in whom you confide.

_____ **20.** Groups of people the same age are called *peer groups*.

_____ **21.** Tobacco, alcohol, and other drugs *strengthen* your ability to make sound decisions.

_____ **22.** *Agreeing* to participate in high-risk behavior is called abstinence.

_____ **23.** Being *assertive* means not giving in to others when you think something is wrong.

_____ **24.** Assertive people have *less control* over their lives.

_____ **25.** One way to deal with a bully is to *walk away*.

Name_____Date_____Class_____

Communicating With Others

MATCHING

Directions: Match each definition in the left column with the correct term from the right column. Write the letter of the term in the space provided. Do not use any term more than once.

Definitions

_____ **1.** Ways that you select, organize, and interpret information

_____ **2.** Talking about people and their personal lives

_____ **3.** Talking about a conflict and deciding how to reach a compromise

_____ **4.** Process by which peers help students find a solution to a conflict

_____ **5.** An agreement in which each person gives up something in order to reach a solution

_____ **6.** The process of sending and receiving messages

_____ **7.** The use of gestures and body movements to communicate a message

_____ **8.** A disagreement, struggle, or fight

_____ **9.** The response given to a message sent

_____ **10.** An opinion about people that is formed without facts or knowledge

Terms

A. negotiation
B. compromise
C. conflict
D. gossip
E. body language
F. prejudice
G. peer mediation
H. communication
I. feedback
J. perceptions

MULTIPLE CHOICE

Directions: In the space provided, write the letter of the choice that BEST completes the statement or answers the question.

_____ **11.** All of the following are effective ways to communicate EXCEPT __?__.
   A. talk about your own experiences and feelings
   B. assume that your listener knows what you want
   C. use a tone of voice that reveals your feelings
   D. check that your listener understands what you say

(Continued on next page)

Chapter 4 Test continued

_____ 12. Which of the following is NOT an example of nonverbal communication?
    A. whispering
    B. gestures
    C. posture
    D. physical appearance

_____ 13. All of the following are ways to improve your listening skills EXCEPT __?__.
    A. concentrate on what the speaker is saying
    B. listen for the overall meaning
    C. interrupt whenever you have a question
    D. give feedback to show you have understood

_____ 14. When you respond to show that you have understood a message, you are providing __?__.
    A. distraction
    B. feedback
    C. judgment
    D. gossip

_____ 15. All of the following are effective ways of resolving conflict EXCEPT __?__.
    A. state your viewpoint as clearly as possible
    B. listen carefully to what the other person has to say
    C. use body language to communicate your feelings
    D. make your point by using sentences starting with "you"

FILL IN THE BLANK

Directions: In the space provided, write the word (or words) that BEST completes each sentence.

_____ 16. If your tone of voice does not match what you are saying, you may send a __?__. *(2 words)*

_____ 17. Conflicts often occur when people don't __?__ effectively.

_____ 18. Conflicts involving __?__ occur when people judge others without getting to know them.

_____ 19. Negotiation involves talking about a conflict in order to reach a __?__.

_____ 20. Some people need a __?__, who is not involved in the conflict, to help them reach a compromise. *(2 words)*

Chapter 5 Test

Citizenship & Leadership

MATCHING

Directions: Match each definition in the left column with the correct term from the right column. Write the letter of the term in the space provided. Do not use any term more than once.

Definitions

_____ **1.** lacking interest or concern

_____ **2.** person who donates time and energy to help others

_____ **3.** person with the ability to guide and motivate others

_____ **4.** accepting of different opinions and ideas

_____ **5.** guidance that helps a group meet its goals

_____ **6.** member of a community such as a city or state

_____ **7.** the way you handle your community responsibilities

_____ **8.** work done by people who cooperate to reach a goal

Terms

A. apathetic
B. citizen
C. citizenship
D. leader
E. leadership
F. teamwork
G. tolerant
H. volunteer

FILL IN THE BLANK

Directions: In the space provided, write the word (or words) that BEST completes each sentence.

_____ **9.** A __?__ has the right to vote in his or her community.

_____ **10.** When you volunteer to help others you __?__ to the community.

_____ **11.** To motivate others, leaders need good __?__ skills.

_____ **12.** A team operates effectively when all of the members __?__.

_____ **13.** You might want to encourage an apathetic person to __?__. *(2 words)*

_____ **14.** It is good manners to __?__ if you make a mistake.

(Continued on next page)

Discovering Life Skills • Teacher Resource Guide
Copyright © Glencoe/McGraw-Hill

Chapter 5 Test continued

MULTIPLE CHOICE

Directions: In the space provided, write the letter of the choice that BEST completes the statement or answers the question.

_____ **15.** The benefits of volunteering include all of the following EXCEPT __?__.
A. it helps you feel good about yourself
B. you make some extra money
C. you gain valuable experience
D. you enjoy a sense of accomplishment

_____ **16.** In order to accomplish its goals, every group needs a __?__.
A. mentor
B. coach
C. volunteer
D. leader

_____ **17.** To be a good leader, do all of the following EXCEPT __?__.
A. do the most difficult tasks yourself
B. keep a positive attitude about all tasks
C. get the facts before making a decision
D. set a good example and be encouraging

_____ **18.** When working as part of a team, do all of the following EXCEPT __?__.
A. show respect to other team members
B. try to persuade others to your point of view
C. stay positive and focused on the goal
D. be ready to compliment other team members

_____ **19.** An apathetic person is someone who __?__.
A. lacks interest or concern
B. feels sorry for you
C. works well in a team
D. makes hateful comments

_____ **20.** All of the following are ways to show good manners EXCEPT __?__.
A. if someone is speaking, don't interrupt
B. if you knock something over, pick it up
C. if you're in a hurry, cut in line
D. if you bump into someone, say "Excuse me"

Discovering Life Skills • Teacher Resource Guide
Copyright © Glencoe/McGraw-Hill

Managing Your Life

MATCHING

Directions: Match each definition in the left column with the correct term from the right column. Write the letter of the term in the space provided. Do not use any term more than once. Some terms will not be used.

Definitions

_____ **1.** Choices about what actions to take

_____ **2.** The results of the choices you make

_____ **3.** Something you want to achieve

_____ **4.** Something you give up in order to get something more important

_____ **5.** Goals that take a long time to reach

_____ **6.** Goals that can be reached relatively quickly

_____ **7.** Different options to consider when making decisions

_____ **8.** The way you feel about something

Terms

A. alternatives
B. attitude
C. consequences
D. decisions
E. goal
F. long-term goals
G. priorities
H. responsibility
I. short-term goals
J. trade-off

FILL IN THE BLANK

Directions: In the space provided, write the word (or words) that BEST completes each sentence.

_____ **9.** If you know what is important to you, you'll find it easier to make __?__ and figure out how to reach them.

_____ **10.** Personal goals help you __?__ the things you want in life.

_____ **11.** Short-term goals can be reached more __?__ than long-term goals.

_____ **12.** It's important to set goals that are __?__ so that you can reach them.

(Continued on next page)

Chapter 6 Test *continued*

_____ **13.** When making a plan, a good first step is to __?__ your goals. *(2 words)*

_____ **14.** Time, skills, and energy are examples of __?__ you can use to reach your goals.

_____ **15.** A __?__ attitude helps you do your best and achieve your goals.

_____ **16.** When making decisions, you need to examine your __?__, or choices.

_____ **17.** You learn from a decision by __?__ it after you act on it.

_____ **18.** When you make a decision, you must also accept __?__ for it.

TRUE/FALSE

Directions: Read each statement carefully. If the statement is true, place a plus (+) in the space provided. If the statement is false, replace the italicized word(s) with the correct word(s). Write your answer in the space provided.

_____ **19.** For a young teen, going to college is an example of a *short-term goal*.

_____ **20.** Your goals need to be *challenging* so that you stay interested in reaching them.

_____ **21.** A *priority* is something you give up in order to get something more important.

_____ **22.** A decision in which you weigh all the facts is a *default decision*.

_____ **23.** When making a decision, you need to list all the *alternatives*.

_____ **24.** When making a decision, your should *avoid taking risks*.

_____ **25.** Accepting the consequences of your decisions is a sign of *maturity*.

Chapter 7
Test

Exploring Careers

MATCHING

Directions: Match each definition in the left column with the correct term from the right column. Write the letter of the term in the space provided. Do not use any term more than once.

Definitions

_____ **1.** Natural abilities or talents

_____ **2.** An organization made up of people employed in a field

_____ **3.** A person who starts and runs his or her own business

_____ **4.** Training that combines coursework and work experience

_____ **5.** Making use of personal connections to achieve your goals

Terms

A. apprenticeship program
B. aptitudes
C. entrepreneur
D. networking
E. professional organization

FILL IN THE BLANK

Directions: In the space provided, write the word (or words) that BEST completes each sentence.

_____ **6.** The first step in making a __?__ is to list all the careers that interest you. *(2 words)*

_____ **7.** When considering a career, think about your __?__, or what is important to you.

_____ **8.** A(n) __?__ test predicts your ability to learn certain skills.

_____ **9.** The most direct way of finding a job is by __?__ with people you know.

_____ **10.** Professional organizations charge a __?__, but offer a variety of helpful services. *(2 words)*

_____ **11.** Job opportunities for people without a high school education are very __?__.

(Continued on next page)

Discovering Life Skills • Teacher Resource Guide
Copyright © Glencoe/McGraw-Hill

Chapter 7 Test *continued*

_____ **12.** An apprenticeship program combines coursework with
_____?____. *(2 words)*

_____ **13.** One of the advantages of running your own business is
that you are your own ___?___.

MULTIPLE CHOICE

Directions: In the space provided, write the letter of the choice that BEST completes the statement
or answers the question.

_____ **14.** When making a career plan, do all of the following EXCEPT ___?___.
   A. list all the careers that interest you
   B. gather information about each career
   C. choose the career that seems easiest
   D. review your plan and modify it as needed

_____ **15.** Which of the following are good people to network with?
   A. friends and relatives   **C.** employers and coworkers
   B. teachers and mentors   **D.** all of the above

_____ **16.** Which of the following is NOT a way to continue your education and training
after high school?
   A. attend a college or university
   B. enroll at a career or technical center
   C. post your résumé on the Internet
   D. join a branch of the military

_____ **17.** Part-time work helps you in all of the following ways EXCEPT ___?___.
   A. you learn how to avoid unpleasant tasks
   B. you learn how to get along with coworkers
   C. you gain helpful work experience
   D. you become aware of job requirements

_____ **18.** All of the following are inappropriate ways of using technology at work EXCEPT ___?___.
   A. sending e-mails to your friends   **C.** doing the work assigned to you
   B. playing on-line computer games   **D.** checking the local movie listings

_____ **19.** Entrepreneurs are people who ___?___.
   A. apply for jobs on the Internet   **C.** apply for a raise and a promotion
   B. evaluate employee performance   **D.** start and run their own business

_____ **20.** All of the following are valid reasons for working EXCEPT ___?___.
   A. to use one's skills to earn a living   **C.** to get a feeling of accomplishment
   B. to fill time and avoid boredom   **D.** to meet people and make friends

Chapter 8 Test

Employability Skills

MATCHING

Directions: Match each definition in the left column with the correct term from the right column. Write the letter of the term in the space provided. Do not use any term more than once. Some terms will not be used.

Definitions

_____ 1. A move into a job with more responsibility

_____ 2. A written record of how well an employee performs on the job

_____ 3. The ability to understand what you read

_____ 4. A personal commitment to do your very best on the job

_____ 5. A summary of an applicant's qualifications, work experience, education, and interests

_____ 6. To leave a job

_____ 7. The ability to adjust easily to new conditions

_____ 8. People who can tell an employer about an applicant's character and work

Terms

A. comprehension
B. promotion
C. references
D. résumé
E. flexibility
F. terminate
G. work ethic
H. work record
I. team

FILL IN THE BLANK

Directions: In the space provided, write the word (or words) that BEST completes each sentence.

_____ 9. You can use a dictionary to build your __?__ and develop your reading skills.

_____ 10. SQ3R stands for Survey, Question, Read, Recite, and __?__.

_____ 11. Improve your writing skills by taking time to __?__ your thoughts.

_____ 12. Improve your speaking skills by learning to __?__ words clearly and correctly.

(Continued on next page)

Chapter 8 Test *continued*

_____ **13.** Improve your listening skills by __?__ on what the other person is saying.

_____ **14.** Knowing how to use a __?__ is essential in today's workplace.

MULTIPLE CHOICE

Directions: In the space provided, write the letter of the choice that BEST completes the statement or answers the question.

_____ **15.** When filling out a job application, do all of the following EXCEPT __?__.
  A. read the application form carefully
  B. print neatly using blue or black ink
  C. cross out any questions that do not apply
  D. make sure you have answered every question

_____ **16.** Which of these people should you NOT use as a reference?
  A. teacher
  B. previous employer
  C. religious leader
  D. best friend

_____ **17.** After going for a job interview, you should follow up by __?__.
  A. sending a thank you note
  B. telephoning the next day
  C. asking additional questions
  D. avoiding further contact

_____ **18.** Being part of a team at work requires __?__.
  A. leadership skills
  B. cooperation with others
  C. performance reviews
  D. self evaluation

_____ **19.** A work record may contain __?__.
  A. how well you fulfilled your responsibilities
  B. how often you were late or missed work
  C. comments about your attitude
  D. all of the above

_____ **20.** If you decide to leave a job, be sure to __?__.
  A. give at least two weeks notice
  B. provide a letter of resignation
  C. state the exact date you will leave
  D. all of the above

Chapter Test 9

Caring for Children

MATCHING

Directions: Match each definition in the left column with the correct term from the right column. Write the letter of the term in the space provided. Do not use any term more than once. Some terms will not be used.

Definitions

Terms

A. attention span
B. child abuse
C. child neglect
D. consistency
E. cooperative play
F. developmental tasks
G. discipline
H. guidance
I. independent play
J. parenthood

_____ 1. Achievements that can be expected at various ages and stages of growth

_____ 2. Play during which an infant shows little interest in interacting with other children

_____ 3. The length of time a person can concentrate on any one thing

_____ 4. Play that involves two or more children and sharing of toys

_____ 5. The function of being a parent

_____ 6. Physical, emotional, or sexual injury to a child

_____ 7. The task of teaching a child which behavior is acceptable and which is not

_____ 8. Direction aimed at teaching children basic rules for behavior

FILL IN THE BLANK

Directions: In the space provided, write the word (or words) that BEST completes each sentence.

_____ 9. __?__ is the process of caring for children and helping them grow and learn.

_____ 10. Children's __?__ needs include healthful food, clothing, rest, sleep, and a safe environment.

_____ 11. Reading books and playing with puzzles and blocks help develop a child's __?__ abilities.

(Continued on next page)

Discovering Life Skills • Teacher Resource Guide
Copyright © Glencoe/McGraw-Hill

Chapter 9 Test continued

_____ **12.** Emphasizing what children are allowed to do rather than what they should not do is a way of focusing on the __?__.

_____ **13.** You are __?__ when you react the same way to a situation each time it occurs.

_____ **14.** Child __?__ is failure to meet a child's physical and emotional needs.

_____ **15.** A child should never be left with someone who is not __?__

MULTIPLE CHOICE

Directions: In the space provided, write the letter of the choice that BEST completes the statement or answers the question.

_____ **16.** Which of the following can you expect newborn babies to do?
- **A.** eat every few hours
- **B.** play with toys
- **C.** follow a set schedule
- **D.** sleep all night

_____ **17.** A toddler's frequent use of the word "no" is related to __?__.
- **A.** following simple rules
- **B.** gaining approval
- **C.** becoming independent
- **D.** learning to disobey

_____ **18.** All of the following are good toys for infants EXCEPT __?__.
- **A.** musical toys
- **B.** action toys
- **C.** squeeze toys
- **D.** nesting blocks

_____ **19.** Which of the following is NOT typical of toddlers' play?
- **A.** they play alone or watch others
- **B.** they readily share and take turns
- **C.** they like toys that move
- **D.** they like to use their imagination

_____ **20.** The benefits of play for preschoolers include all of the following EXCEPT __?__.
- **A.** taking turns
- **B.** sharing with others
- **C.** making friends
- **D.** taking control

Babysitting Basics

MATCHING

Directions: Match each definition in the left column with the correct term from the right column. Write the letter of the term in the space provided. Do not use any term more than once.

Definitions

_____ **1.** Someone who uses force to get into a home

_____ **2.** Containing no poisonous or harmful substances

_____ **3.** Suitable for a child of a particular age

_____ **4.** To turn someone's attention to something else

_____ **5.** Safe for children to play and explore in

_____ **6.** Able to be depended upon

_____ **7.** Steps taken to avoid danger

Terms

A. age-appropriate
B. childproof
C. intruder
D. nontoxic
E. precautions
F. redirect
G. reliable

FILL IN THE BLANK

Directions: In the space provided, write the word (or words) that BEST completes each sentence.

_____ **8.** When parents make their home __?__, they make the home safe for children to explore.

_____ **9.** A __?__ is a device that prevents children from opening cabinets and drawers. *(2 words)*

_____ **10.** Because babies put small objects in their mouth, anything small enough to be __?__ should be placed out of their reach.

_____ **11.** You can learn how to take care of basic injuries by taking a __?__ course.

_____ **12.** To prevent fires, make sure there are __?__ on every floor of the home. *(2 words)*

(Continued on next page)

Chapter 10 Test *continued*

_____ **13.** If you suspect a child has been poisoned, call the __?__ center immediately. *(2 words)*

_____ **14.** When you are holding an infant, be sure to support his or her __?__.

_____ **15.** Babies should never be laid on their __?__ to sleep.

_____ **16.** You can often comfort toddlers by __?__ their attention to something else.

_____ **17.** When babysitting preschoolers, you need to plan lots of __?__ to keep them entertained.

TRUE/FALSE

Directions: Read each statement carefully. If the statement is true, place a plus (+) in the space provided. If the statement is false, replace the italicized word(s) with the correct word(s). Write your answer in the space provided.

_____ **18.** Children *do not understand* the dangers that surround them.

_____ **19.** Keeping children safe involves protecting them from *intruders*.

_____ **20.** *Fires* are the leading cause of accidental death in the home.

_____ **21.** Make sure that all poisonous substances are stored in a *bathroom* cabinet.

_____ **22.** The first time you babysit for a family, ask the parents to go over the *family rules*.

_____ **23.** If you need to change a diaper, assemble everything you need *after* undressing the baby.

_____ **24.** Most toddlers need to be *ignored* when their parents leave.

_____ **25.** When babysitting preschoolers, remember that they like to be kept *busy*.

Name_____Date_____Class_____

Chapter 11 Test

Managing Your Money

MATCHING

Directions: Match each definition in the left column with the correct term from the right column. Write the letter of the term in the space provided. Do not use any term more than once. Some terms will not be used.

Definitions

_____ **1.** Taking items from a store without paying for them

_____ **2.** A person who buys goods and services

_____ **3.** A plan for using your money

_____ **4.** A method of payment in which you buy now and pay later

_____ **5.** The return of your money in exchange for an item you purchased

_____ **6.** A manufacturer's written promise to repair or replace a faulty product

_____ **7.** A message that persuades consumers to buy a product or service

_____ **8.** The money you spend to buy goods and services

_____ **9.** Action taken to correct a wrong

_____ **10.** The amount of money you earn or receive regularly

Terms

A. advertisement
B. budget
C. consumer
D. credit
E. debit
F. endorsement
G. expenses
H. income
I. redress
J. refund
K. shoplifting
L. warranty
M. comparison shopping

MULTIPLE CHOICE

Directions: In the space provided, write the letter of the choice that BEST completes the statement or answers the question.

_____ **11.** Advertisements are designed to do all of the following EXCEPT __?__.
   A. convince consumers to buy a product or service
   B. provide complete and unbiased information
   C. present goods or services in an attractive way
   D. catch the attention of potential buyers

(Continued on next page)

Chapter 11 Test continued

_____ **12.** A __?__ card enables you to buy now and pay later.
   A. credit
   B. debit
   C. discount
   D. product

_____ **13.** Buying candy while standing in the checkout line is an example of __?__.
   A. decision making
   B. impulse buying
   C. product testing
   D. emotional appeal

_____ **14.** A store that carries only one manufacturer's products is called a __?__.
   A. factory outlet
   B. department store
   C. specialty store
   D. chain store

_____ **15.** To manage your money wisely, you should __?__.
   A. determine how much money you will have
   B. look at how much money you spend
   C. evaluate the products and service you buy
   D. all of the above

FILL IN THE BLANK

Directions: In the space provided, write the word (or words) that BEST completes each sentence.

_____ **16.** If you have a problem with a product that you purchase, you have the right to seek __?__.

_____ **17.** Shoplifting is a serious __?__.

_____ **18.** To receive an exchange or refund, you will need to show your __?__.

_____ **19.** When you manage your money well, you do not spend more on __?__ than you receive in income.

_____ **20.** A __?__ is used to withdraw money directly from a person's bank account. *(2 words)*

Managing Your Resources

MATCHING

Directions: Match each definition in the left column with the correct term from the right column. Write the letter of the term in the space provided. Do not use any term more than once.

Definitions

Terms

_____ **1.** The body's reaction to changes around it

_____ **2.** Using what you have to get what you want

_____ **3.** To determine the value of what you have accomplished

_____ **4.** To rank in order of importance

_____ **5.** To put things off

_____ **6.** Information or expertise that can help you meet your goals

A. evaluate
B. management
C. prioritize
D. procrastinate
E. resource
F. stress

FILL IN THE BLANK

Directions: In the space provided, write the word (or words) that BEST completes each sentence.

_____ **7.** Writing down your goal helps you __?__ to it.

_____ **8.** Evaluating the outcome of a plan helps you determine if you were __?__ with the results.

_____ **9.** The three main types of resources are personal, __?__, and community resources.

_____ **10.** The encouragement of family and friends can help you gain __?__.

_____ **11.** Schools, hospitals, and police services are examples of __?__ resources.

_____ **12.** When you prioritize tasks, you rank them in order of __?__.

(Continued on next page)

Chapter 12 Test *continued*

_____ **13.** To make a task go faster, get __?__ before you begin.

_____ **14.** When you need to study, avoid __?__ such as the television and telephone.

_____ **15.** You may break a long-term goal into several smaller, __?__ goals that are easier to reach.

MULTIPLE CHOICE

Directions: In the space provided, write the letter of the choice that BEST completes the statement or answers the question.

_____ **16.** All of the following are examples of personal resources EXCEPT __?__.
   A. tasks
   B. energy
   C. knowledge
   D. time

_____ **17.** An example of a community resource is a __?__.
   A. town house
   B. public park
   C. driver's license
   D. department store

_____ **18.** Time management skills enable you to do all of the following EXCEPT __?__.
   A. make a choice between two things you want to do
   B. rank your tasks in order of importance
   C. avoid doing anything you don't really want to do
   D. deal with unexpected changes as they arise

_____ **19.** When you procrastinate, you __?__.
   A. make a "to-do" list
   B. remove distractions
   C. put things off until later
   D. set the atmosphere

_____ **20.** All of the following are tips for managing stress EXCEPT __?__.
   A. plan ahead for events you can anticipate
   B. take deep breaths to calm yourself down
   C. exercise by riding a bike or walking
   D. try to forget whatever is troubling you

Your Living Space

MATCHING

Directions: Match each definition in the left column with the correct term from the right column. Write the letter of the term in the space provided. Do not use any term more than once.

Definitions

Terms

A. accessories
B. design
C. floor plan
D. functional
E. texture
F. traffic pattern

_____ 1. Interesting items added to make a space more personal

_____ 2. The path people take to move around and enter and exit a room

_____ 3. Useful and convenient

_____ 4. The art of combining elements in a pleasing way

_____ 5. The way something feels or looks as if it would feel

_____ 6. A drawing of a room and how its furniture is arranged

MULTIPLE CHOICE

Directions: In the space provided, write the letter of the choice that BEST completes the statement or answers the question.

_____ 7. Homes are usually divided into living areas that serve more than one __?__.
   A. design
   B. function
   C. address
   D. style

_____ 8. The traffic pattern is __?__.
   A. the main purpose that the room serves
   B. the way furniture is arranged in groups
   C. a method of storing related items
   D. the path people take to move around a room

(Continued on next page)

Chapter 13 Test continued

_____ 9. When organizing the furniture in a room, do all of the following EXCEPT __?__.
   A. place all the large items against the walls
   B. leave space around furniture
   C. place furniture in functional groupings
   D. group related items together

_____ 10. Which of the following lines make objects appear soft and graceful?
   A. diagonal lines   C. straight lines
   B. curved lines   D. horizontal lines

_____ 11. Which of the following design elements has the greatest effect on the appearance of a room?
   A. line   C. color
   B. shape   D. texture

_____ 12. Which of the following colors would NOT be appropriate for a room that gets a lot of sunlight?
   A. blue   C. violet
   B. green   D. orange

_____ 13. All of the following are principles of design EXCEPT __?__.
   A. balance   C. rhythm
   B. proportion   D. style

FILL IN THE BLANK

Directions: In the space provided, write the word (or words) that BEST completes each sentence.

_____ 14. Clothes and other possessions last __?__ if you take care of them.

_____ 15. A __?__ can help families manage their routine cleaning tasks. *(2 words)*

_____ 16. Protect your home from fire by installing __?__ and checking them monthly. *(2 words)*

_____ 17. To prevent falls, use __?__ pads under small rugs so that they won't slide.

_____ 18. Stairs should have handrails and should be kept free of __?__.

_____ 19. Do not give out any __?__ when using the Internet. *(2 words)*

_____ 20. Make sure your hands are __?__ before you connect or disconnect an electrical appliance.

Discovering Life Skills • Teacher Resource Guide
Copyright © Glencoe/McGraw-Hill

Name_____Date_____Class_____

Your Environment

MATCHING

Directions: Match each definition in the left column with the correct term from the right column. Write the letter of the term in the space provided. Do not use any term more than once. Some terms will not be used.

Definitions

Terms

_____ 1. Turning waste items into products that can be used

_____ 2. Huge pits where waste is buried between layers of earth

_____ 3. Material installed in a building to keep it cooler or warmer

_____ 4. To break down and become part of the soil

_____ 5. Disposing of waste by burning it

_____ 6. Able to be broken down and absorbed by the environment

_____ 7. Unable to be replaced once used

_____ 8. Materials that are supplied by nature

_____ 9. Dirty and unsafe air, water, and land

_____ 10. The saving of resources

A. biodegradable
B. conservation
C. decompose
D. environment
E. energy-efficient
F. incineration
G. insulation
H. landfills
I. natural resources
J. nonrenewable
K. pollution
L. recycling

FILL IN THE BLANK

Directions: In the space provided, write the word (or words) that BEST completes each sentence.

_____ 11. If __?__ resources are used up or permanently damaged, they will no longer be available.

_____ 12. Dust, smoke, and chemical particles are all forms of __?__ that can harm your health. *(2 words)*

_____ 13. Uranium, found in rocks, is used to produce __?__ energy.

(Continued on next page)

Discovering Life Skills • Teacher Resource Guide
Copyright © Glencoe/McGraw-Hill

Chapter 14 Test continued

_____ **14.** People who practice __?__ help to save the earth's resources.

_____ **15.** Conserve water by running the washing machine only with a __?__. *(2 words)*

_____ **16.** One way to limit waste is to __?__ the amount of waste you create.

_____ **17.** Turning newspapers into pulp to make new paper is an example of __?__.

_____ **18.** When riding in a car, protect yourself by always wearing a __?__. *(2 words)*

_____ **19.** The best way to protect yourself when participating in water sports is to know how to __?__.

_____ **20.** When people pair up and look out for each other during activities, they are using the __?__ system.

TRUE/FALSE

Directions: Read each statement carefully. If the statement is true, place a plus (+) in the space provided. If the statement is false, replace the italicized word(s) with the correct word(s). Write your answer in the space provided.

_____ **21.** *Water* is your body's most essential nutrient.

_____ **22.** Most of the energy used in the home is for *lighting and cooking.*

_____ **23.** Most waste in the United States is disposed of in *incinerators.*

_____ **24.** *Biodegradable* products break down and are absorbed by the environment.

_____ **25.** You can limit the amount of waste you create by *refilling* items that might otherwise be thrown away.

Chapter 15 Test

Your Fashion Statement

MATCHING

Directions: Match each definition in the left column with the correct term from the right column. Write the letter of the term in the space provided. Do not use any term more than once.

Definitions

Terms

_____ **1.** The name of a color

_____ **2.** The way something feels or looks as if it would feel

_____ **3.** Level of importance

_____ **4.** Fashions that are very popular for a short time

_____ **5.** A light value of a hue

_____ **6.** The brightness or dullness of a color

_____ **7.** Styles of clothing that are accepted as popular

_____ **8.** The design of a garment

_____ **9.** Styles that remain in fashion for a long time

_____ **10.** A dark value of a hue

A. classic
B. fads
C. fashions
D. hue
E. intensity
F. shade
G. status
H. style
I. texture
J. tint

MULTIPLE CHOICE

Directions: In the space provided, write the letter of the choice that BEST completes the statement or answers the question.

_____ **11.** All of the following are primary colors EXCEPT __?__.
A. red
B. green
C. yellow
D. blue

(Continued on next page)

Chapter 15 Test continued

_____ **12.** Which of the following indicates the brightness or dullness of a color?
    A. hue
    B. tint
    C. shade
    D. intensity

_____ **13.** Which of the following is NOT considered a warm color?
    A. green
    B. red
    C. orange
    D. yellow

_____ **14.** Which color scheme is made up of hues found next to each other on the color wheel?
    A. monochromatic
    B. complementary
    C. analogous
    D. accented neutral

_____ **15.** Which of the following is an example of a complementary color scheme?
    A. orange and blue
    B. red and white
    C. blue and green
    D. yellow and orange

FILL IN THE BLANK

Directions: In the space provided, write the word (or words) that BEST completes each sentence.

_____ **16.** When people choose clothing to keep themselves warm in cold weather, they are choosing clothing for __?__.

_____ **17.** It is not a good idea to spend a lot of money on __?__ clothing, because it quickly loses its appeal.

_____ **18.** The __?__ or activity for which you are dressing helps to determine your clothing choices.

_____ **19.** If you want to look taller and thinner, choose clothing with __?__ lines.

_____ **20.** You can give an outfit a different look with some well-chosen __?__.

Clothing Basics

MATCHING

Directions: Match each definition in the left column with the correct term from the right column. Write the letter of the term in the space provided. Do not use any term more than once.

Definitions

_____ **1.** Fabrics that will keep their original color through many washings

_____ **2.** A trademark used by a manufacturer to identify its products

_____ **3.** Fabrics made by interlacing lengthwise and crosswise threads

_____ **4.** The direction the threads run in a fabric

_____ **5.** Tiny strands that make up the threads used to make fabrics

_____ **6.** A strategy for spending money to purchase items you need or want

_____ **7.** Made partially or entirely from chemicals

_____ **8.** Fabrics made by looping threads together

Terms

A. brand name
B. colorfast fabrics
C. fibers
D. grain
E. knit fabrics
F. shopping plan
G. synthetic
H. woven fabrics

FILL IN THE BLANK

Directions: In the space provided, write the word (or words) that BEST completes each sentence.

_____ **9.** Fabric that springs back when stretched or crushed is __?__ fabric.

_____ **10.** Cotton, linen, silk, and wool are made from __?__ fibers.

_____ **11.** Polyester and nylon are examples of __?__ fibers.

_____ **12.** The fiber content of a garment is described on the __?__. *(2 words)*

(Continued on next page)

Chapter 16 Test continued

_____ **13.** The denim used to make jeans is an example of a __?__ weave.

_____ **14.** Sweaters are made from __?__ fabrics.

_____ **15.** Manufacturers often add __?__ to improve the durability or quality of fabrics.

MULTIPLE CHOICE

Directions: In the space provided, write the letter of the choice that BEST completes the statement or answers the question.

_____ **16.** Quality clothing has all of the following characteristics EXCEPT __?__.
- **A.** cut on grain
- **B.** springs back when stretched
- **C.** springs back when crushed
- **D.** cut off grain

_____ **17.** The labels in a garment will tell you all of the following EXCEPT _____.
- **A.** fiber content and name of manufacturer
- **B.** the correct way to wash the garment
- **C.** what to do if the garment does not fit
- **D.** whether or not the garment should be ironed

_____ **18.** All of the following are good ways to stretch your clothing budget EXCEPT _____.
- **A.** always buy the latest fashions
- **B.** make the best use of what you have
- **C.** take good care of your clothes
- **D.** start with two or three basic outfits

_____ **19.** Which of the following is NOT a good way to care for your clothing?
- **A.** dress and undress carefully
- **B.** inspect your clothes after each wearing
- **C.** repair tears and holes before they get bigger
- **D.** leave stained clothes for a day before treating them

_____ **20.** When washing your clothes, do all of the following EXCEPT _____.
- **A.** pretreat stains, sleeve cuffs, and collars
- **B.** sort clothes by color and fabric
- **C.** pack the clothes tightly in the washer
- **D.** select the correct water temperature

Preparing to Sew

MATCHING

Directions: Match each definition in the left column with the correct term from the right column. Write the letter of the term in the space provided. Do not use any term more than once.

Definitions

_____ **1.** A one-way texture in a fabric

_____ **2.** Items you need to complete a sewing project

_____ **3.** A plan for making a garment or project

_____ **4.** A version of a garment style shown on a pattern envelope

_____ **5.** Tapered V-shaped seams used to give a garment shape

_____ **6.** A change made in a pattern to make a garment fit

Terms

A. alteration
B. darts
C. nap
D. notions
E. pattern
F. view

MULTIPLE CHOICE

Directions: In the space provided, write the letter of the choice that BEST completes the statement or answers the question.

_____ **7.** __?__ give shape to a garment.
   A. arrows
   B. darts
   C. seams
   D. dots

_____ **8.** A(n) __?__ is a plan for making a garment or project.
   A. notion
   B. pattern
   C. alteration
   D. interfacing

(Continued on next page)

Chapter 17 Test continued

_____   **9.** All of the following are notions EXCEPT __?__.
      A. thread
      B. buttons
      C. zippers
      D. fabric

_____   **10.** The label on the end of a bolt of fabric gives facts about __?__.
      A. fiber content, finishes, shrinkage, and care
      B. types of garments for which the fabric is suitable
      C. suggested notions and interfacing to use
      D. number of yards needed for specific projects

_____   **11.** When choosing a fabric, ask yourself all of these questions EXCEPT __?__.
      A. When will the item be used?
      B. How will the item be used?
      C. Which fabric is most expensive?
      D. What kind of care does it need?

_____   **12.** Which of the following is NOT a safety tip for using an iron?
      A. Test the heat of the iron on silk fabric.
      B. Always rest the iron on its heel.
      C. Unplug the iron when you finish using it.
      D. Coil the cord so that no one can trip over it.

FILL IN THE BLANK

Directions: In the space provided, write the word (or words) that BEST completes each sentence.

_____ **13.** When you return a sewing lab item to the correct place after using it, you show __?__ for others.

_____ **14.** If you have little sewing experience, you should choose a(n) __?__ pattern.

_____ **15.** When taking bust or chest, waist, and hip measurements, make sure the measuring tape is held __?__ to the floor.

_____ **16.** Corduroy is an example of a fabric with __?__, or a one-way texture.

_____ **17.** When you finish ironing, you should __?__ the iron.

_____ **18.** Zippers, buttons, and snaps are all examples of __?__.

_____ **19.** Interfacing is used to give more __?__ to a garment.

_____ **20.** Thread should be the same color as the fabric, or slightly __?__.

Sewing & Serging Basics

MATCHING

Directions: Match each definition in the left column with the correct term from the right column. Write the letter of the term in the space provided. Do not use any term more than once. Some terms will not be used.

Definitions

Terms

_____ 1. Printed guides on pattern pieces

_____ 2. Fabric tunnels made to enclose elastic or drawstrings

_____ 3. Large cylinders used to hold thread on a serger

_____ 4. A row of stitching made on or very near the seam line

_____ 5. The tightly woven edge of fabric that has no loose threads

_____ 6. Diagrams of how pattern pieces should be placed on fabric

_____ 7. Rounded parts that hold the thread inside a serger

_____ 8. The diagonal on a piece of fabric

_____ 9. A set of step-by-step instructions for sewing a pattern

_____ 10. Fullness added to a garment pattern for movement and comfort

A. bias
B. casings
C. cones
D. ease
E. guide sheet
F. layouts
G. loopers
H. markings
I. seam gauge
J. selvage
K. serger
L. staystitching

MULTIPLE CHOICE

Directions: In the space provided, write the letter of the choice that BEST completes the statement or answers the question.

_____ 11. A guide sheet contains all of the following EXCEPT __?__.
    A. general information on how to use the pattern
    B. a list of recommended fabrics and notions
    C. a diagram of all the pattern pieces
    D. an explanation of the pattern markings

(Continued on next page)

Chapter 18 Test *continued*

_____ **12.** When pinning pattern pieces to fabric, do all of the following EXCEPT __?__.
   A. place pins only along the fold line
   B. place pins about 1 inch apart
   C. place pins along the cutting line
   D. place pins about 2 inches apart

_____ **13.** When you begin to sew a garment, the first step is to __?__.
   A. stitch the darts
   B. staystitch the seams
   C. stitch the straight seams
   D. stitch the curved seams

_____ **14.** Facings are used to __?__.
   A. finish the raw edges of a garment
   B. enclose elastic or drawstrings
   C. create fullness without puckering
   D. hold overlapping edges together

_____ **15.** A serger is a high-speed machine that __?__.
   A. sews a single line of locked stitches
   B. replaces a conventional sewing machine
   C. sews on buttons, snaps, and hooks and eyes
   D. sews, trims, and finishes a seam in one step

FILL IN THE BLANK

Directions: In the space provided, write the word (or words) that BEST completes each sentence.

_____ **16.** After preshrinking your fabric, you should make sure it is straight by checking the __?__.

_____ **17.** If you need to make alterations to a pattern, you should do so __?__ you cut the fabric.

_____ **18.** You should cut around the __?__ of the notches on your pattern.

_____ **19.** You can prevent fabric from raveling at the seams by adding a __?__. *(2 words)*

_____ **20.** The purpose of __?__ is to attach a longer piece of fabric to a shorter one, and achieve a soft, full effect.

Chapter 19 Test

Expressing Creativity

MATCHING

Directions: Match each definition in the left column with the correct term from the right column. Write the letter of the term in the space provided. Do not use any term more than once.

Definitions

_____ **1.** A means of release or satisfaction

_____ **2.** Ability to use imagination and art forms to create something

_____ **3.** A triangle- or diamond-shaped piece of fabric used to widen pant legs

_____ **4.** Interesting items added to make an outfit or a room more personal

_____ **5.** Decorative fabric cutout that can be stitched or glued to a garment

Terms

A. accessories
B. appliqué
C. creativity
D. gusset
E. outlet

FILL IN THE BLANK

Directions: In the space provided, write the word (or words) that BEST completes each sentence.

_____ **6.** You can express your __?__ with sewing and with a variety of art forms.

_____ **7.** Creativity enables you to express __?__, such as fear or anger, in a healthy way.

_____ **8.** To express your creativity, you need to find the __?__ that is most satisfying to you.

_____ **9.** You can add a creative touch to __?__ such as scarves, caps, and bags.

_____ **10.** Make jeans more interesting by using patterned __?__ to widen the legs.

_____ **11.** A small tear in a garment can be covered by a decorative __?__ .

(Continued on next page)

Chapter 19 Test *continued*

_____ **12.** When setting aside old clothes to use as rags, remove and save the __?__ so that you can use them for other projects.

_____ **13.** When painting a room, you can draw attention to one wall by using an __?__ color.

_____ **14.** Putting shells around a photo taken at the beach is a way of __?__ a picture frame.

MULTIPLE CHOICE

Directions: In the space provided, write the letter of the choice that BEST completes the statement or answers the question.

_____ **15.** Which of the following is NOT a way to express yourself in a creative manner?
  A. write a poem or a story
  B. watch television
  C. draw or paint a picture
  D. make something with your hands

_____ **16.** All of the following are examples of wearable art EXCEPT __?__.
  A. a safety pin strung with colored beads
  B. ankle socks decorated with lace trim
  C. a baseball cap with a colorful appliqué
  D. a photo frame decorated with paper hearts

_____ **17.** When you replace the buttons on a shirt with decorative buttons, you __?__.
  A. make a unique statement about your style
  B. spoil the original look of the garment
  C. show that you value the environment
  D. give your peers an idea to copy

_____ **18.** A triangle- or diamond-shaped piece of fabric used to widen the legs of jeans is a(n) __?__.
  A. appliqué   **C.** embroidery
  B. gusset   **D.** shank

_____ **19.** The first thing you should do when decorating your room is __?__.
  A. stick interesting shapes on the ceiling
  B. paint one of the walls in an accent color
  C. cover the furniture with stick-on shapes
  D. ask your parent or guardian for permission

_____ **20.** All of the following are ways to personalize your room using paint EXCEPT __?__.
  A. paint a scene on one wall
  B. paint a geometric pattern on one wall
  C. use a neutral color on all the walls
  D. use an accent color on one wall

Nutrition & Wellness

MATCHING

Directions: Match each definition in the left column with the correct term from the right column. Write the letter of the term in the space provided. Do not use any term more than once. Some terms will not be used.

Definitions

_____ 1. The process of breaking down food into a form the body can use

_____ 2. The starches and sugars that give the body most of its energy

_____ 3. A waxy substance produced in the body and present in high-fat foods

_____ 4. Substances in food that are important for the body's growth and care

_____ 5. Elements needed in small amounts for healthy bones, teeth, and blood

_____ 6. Nutrients that are needed to build, repair, and maintain body cells and tissues

_____ 7. Substances needed in small quantities to help regulate body functions

_____ 8. Plant material that the body cannot digest

_____ 9. The building blocks that make up protein

_____ 10. A condition in which bones gradually become weak and brittle

Terms

A. amino acids
B. calorie
C. carbohydrates
D. cholesterol
E. digestion
F. fiber
G. minerals
H. nutrients
I. osteoporosis
J. proteins
K. vitamins
L. wellness

(Continued on next page)

Chapter 20 Test continued

FILL IN THE BLANK

Directions: In the space provided, write the word (or words) that BEST completes each sentence.

_____ **11.** Hunger is the need to eat, while __?__ is the desire to eat.

_____ **12.** __?__ are units used to measure the energy in food and the energy used by the body.

_____ **13.** Foods that contain all the essential amino acids are called ___?___. *(2 words)*

_____ **14.** Foods made from whole grain are good sources of __?__.

_____ **15.** Fats that come from plants and that are generally liquid at room temperature are called __?__. *(2 words)*

_____ **16.** You need foods containing __?__ to develop strong bones and teeth.

_____ **17.** Females need about twice as much __?__ as males.

_____ **18.** The __?__ makes it easy to plan healthful meals. *(3 words)*

_____ **19.** Too much __?__ in the diet can contribute to high blood pressure.

_____ **20.** Empty-calorie foods are high in calories but low in __?__ .

TRUE/FALSE

Directions: Read each statement carefully. If the statement is true, place a plus (+) in the space provided. If the statement is false, replace the italicized word(s) with the correct word(s). Write your answer in the space provided.

_____ **21.** *Proteins* are needed to build, repair, and maintain body cells and tissues.

_____ **22.** Dry beans, nuts, and grains are examples of *complete* proteins.

_____ **23.** *Fibers* are the starches and sugars that give your body most of its energy.

_____ **24.** *Fats* contain twice as many calories as carbohydrates.

_____ **25.** *Vitamin D* helps your body heal and fight infection.

Health & Fitness

MATCHING

Directions: Match each definition in the left column with the correct term from the right column. Write the letter of the term in the space provided. Do not use any term more than once. Some terms will not be used.

Definitions

Terms

A. anorexia nervosa
B. binge eating
C. bulimia nervosa
D. eating disorders
E. energy
F. exercise
G. fad diet
H. fitness
I. obesity
J. stamina

_____ **1.** An eating disorder characterized by self-starvation to lose weight

_____ **2.** Extreme eating behaviors that can lead to depression, anxiety, or even death

_____ **3.** A diet that promises quick weight loss through unusual means

_____ **4.** The ability to handle daily events in a healthy way

_____ **5.** An eating disorder characterized by a lack of control over eating habits

_____ **6.** A condition in which a person is 20 percent or more above healthy weight

_____ **7.** An eating disorder characterized by overeating followed by purging

_____ **8.** The ability to focus on a single activity for a long time

FILL IN THE BLANK

Directions: In the space provided, write the word (or words) that BEST completes each sentence.

_____ **9.** When you are __?__, you have enough energy to do your schoolwork and chores, and have fun too. *(2 words)*

_____ **10.** Exercising regularly will help you feel __?__ about yourself.

_____ **11.** People who maintain a __?__ body weight are neither too fat nor too thin.

(Continued on next page)

Chapter 21 Test *continued*

_____ **12.** Eating disorders are __?__ problems related to food.

_____ **13.** To control your weight, you have to balance the __?__ you get from food with those you use for energy.

_____ **14.** Most people who lose weight on a __?__ gain it back again. *(2 words)*

_____ **15.** A sensible approach to weight control is to combine a good diet with __?__.

MULTIPLE CHOICE

Directions: In the space provided, write the letter of the choice that BEST completes the statement or answers the question.

_____ **16.** The benefits of fitness include all of the following EXCEPT __?__.
   A. you feel positive about yourself
   B. you have the energy you need
   C. you are able to eat more
   D. you are able to handle stress

_____ **17.** Which of the following is NOT a good way to keep a healthy body image?
   A. educate yourself about nutrition
   B. keep a positive attitude about yourself
   C. exercise regularly
   D. eat as little as possible

_____ **18.** The key to losing weight is to __?__.
   A. use more calories than you consume
   B. weigh yourself every day
   C. skip meals regularly
   D. go on a fad diet

_____ **19.** Which of the following is NOT a benefit of exercise?
   A. it burns calories
   B. it helps your heart work better
   C. it tones your muscles
   D. it makes you feel hungry

_____ **20.** All of the following are true of fad diets EXCEPT __?__.
   A. they are rarely successful in controlling weight
   B. they don't provide the nutrients you need
   C. they are the best way to lose weight quickly
   D. they may cause physical harm

Working in the Kitchen

MATCHING

Directions: Match each definition in the left column with the correct term from the right column. Write the letter of the term in the space provided. Do not use any term more than once.

Definitions

Terms

A. appliances
B. conduct
C. contamination
D. E. coli
E. flammable
F. perishable
G. salmonella
H. utensils

_____ 1. Becoming infected with harmful bacteria

_____ 2. Likely to spoil quickly

_____ 3. To carry electricity

_____ 4. Small electrically powered items of kitchen equipment

_____ 5. Bacteria found in contaminated water, raw beef, and unpasteurized milk

_____ 6. Bacteria found in raw or undercooked foods such as meat, eggs, and fish

_____ 7. Kitchen tools used for specific tasks

_____ 8. Capable of burning easily

TRUE/FALSE

Directions: Read each statement carefully. If the statement is true, place a plus (+) in the space provided. If the statement is false, replace the italicized word(s) with the correct word(s). Write your answer in the space provided.

_____ 9. Keeping food safe prevents *contamination*.

_____ 10. To protect yourself from E. coli, only eat hamburger that is *well done*.

_____ 11. *Perishable* foods are likely to spoil quickly.

_____ 12. Cooked foods should not be left at room temperature for more than two *days*.

(Continued on next page)

Chapter 22 Test continued

_____ **13.** When freezing leftovers, pack them in an *airtight container*.

_____ **14.** Most kitchen accidents are *preventable*.

MULTIPLE CHOICE

Directions: In the space provided, write the letter of the choice that BEST completes the statement or answers the question.

_____ **15.** Which of the following is NOT a way to prevent falls in the kitchen?
  A. stand on a chair to get at high items
  B. clean up spilled liquids immediately
  C. turn pot handles toward the center of the stove
  D. keep cupboard doors and drawers closed

_____ **16.** To prevent fires in the kitchen, do all of the following EXCEPT __?__.
  A. keep a fire extinguisher handy and know how to use it
  B. keep potholders and kitchen towels near the stove
  C. don't wear clothing with loose-fitting sleeves
  D. don't leave the kitchen while you have food cooking

_____ **17.** Prevent cuts in the kitchen by doing all of the following EXCEPT __?__.
  A. keep knives dull so they won't cut you
  B. use a cutting board for all cutting jobs
  C. wash knives separately from other utensils
  D. store knives in a special compartment

_____ **18.** When using electrical appliances, ALWAYS __?__.
  A. keep appliances unplugged when not in use
  B. dry your hands before touching appliances
  C. use an appliance that has a worn cord
  D. both A and B

_____ **19.** You should always unplug a toaster before trying to pry food from it with a knife because __?__.
  A. the toaster might still be hot
  B. you could get an electric shock
  C. you might cut yourself on the knife
  D. you are more likely to get the food out

_____ **20.** Which of the following is NOT true of large kitchen equipment?
  A. stoves usually come with conventional ovens
  B. conventional ovens may be self-cleaning
  C. conventional ovens use microwaves
  D. some refrigerators are self-defrosting

Preparing to Cook

MATCHING

Directions: Match each definition in the left column with the correct term from the right column. Write the letter of the term in the space provided. Do not use any term more than once.

Definitions

_____ **1.** A habit that determines when and what people eat each day

_____ **2.** A small amount of food or seasoning added to decorate a food

_____ **3.** A dish served before the meal

_____ **4.** The number of servings a recipe will make

_____ **5.** The way food feels when it is eaten

_____ **6.** A list of ingredients and directions for preparing a specific dish

Terms

A. appetizer
B. garnish
C. meal pattern
D. recipe
E. texture
F. yield

FILL IN THE BLANK

Directions: In the space provided, write the word (or words) that BEST completes each sentence.

_____ **7.** When planning meals, choose a combination of foods from the Food Guide Pyramid that fits your __?__. *(2 words)*

_____ **8.** Eating is more interesting if you include a __?__ of foods in your meals.

_____ **9.** Parsley and lemon wedges are examples of __?__ that add more color to a plate.

_____ **10.** When planning meals, consider the __?__ you will need, such as skills, equipment, money, and time.

_____ **11.** When you invite friends over for a meal, ask in advance if anyone has any __?__ needs. *(2 words)*

(Continued on next page)

Discovering Life Skills • Teacher Resource Guide
Copyright © Glencoe/McGraw-Hill

Chapter 23 Test continued

_____ **12.** Food labels must list ingredients in order of ___?___.

_____ **13.** To decide which size of an item is the best buy, check the ___?___ label on the store shelf. *(2 words)*

_____ **14.** When you follow a recipe, it's important that you understand the ___?___, or shortened forms of words.

MULTIPLE CHOICE

Directions: In the space provided, write the letter of the choice that BEST completes the statement or answers the question.

_____ **15.** How many daily servings do you need from the bread, cereal, rice, and pasta group?
    A. two to three
    B. two to four
    C. three to five
    D. six to eleven

_____ **16.** Which of the following is NOT a way to make a meal appealing?
    A. vary the way the foods are prepared
    B. choose foods that are all the same color
    C. vary the sizes and shapes of the foods
    D. choose foods with different textures

_____ **17.** Which of the following are likely to have the lowest cost?
    A. national brands
    B. famous brands
    C. store brands
    D. generic brands

_____ **18.** Food labels must provide all of the following EXCEPT ___?___.
    A. country of origin of the ingredients
    B. the manufacturer's name and address
    C. list of ingredients in order of amount
    D. nutritional content including serving size

_____ **19.** Unit pricing makes price comparisons easier because it ___?___.
    A. tells what size an individual unit is
    B. shows the cost of the product per unit
    C. is displayed on the store shelf
    D. stays the same over time

_____ **20.** All of the following are guidelines for using recipes EXCEPT ___?___.
    A. read through the recipe and make sure you understand it
    B. assemble all the equipment before you start
    C. look for each ingredient when you need it
    D. do any necessary preparation such as greasing a pan

Cooking Basics

MATCHING

Directions: Match each definition in the left column with the correct term from the right column. Write the letter of the term in the space provided. Do not use any term more than once.

Definitions

_____ 1. To bring milk slowly to a temperature just below the boiling point

_____ 2. A main dish pie filled with eggs, cheese, and other ingredients

_____ 3. To separate into tiny particles, or curds

_____ 4. Dry beans and peas

_____ 5. A beaten egg cooked in a frying pan and then topped with other ingredients

_____ 6. Foods that are changed from their raw form before being sold

_____ 7. Foods that are partly prepared to save time

Terms

A. convenience foods
B. curdle
C. legumes
D. omelet
E. processed foods
F. quiche
G. scald

FILL IN THE BLANK

Directions: In the space provided, write the word (or words) that BEST completes each sentence.

_____ 8. A muffin mix is an example of a __?__ that saves time. *(2 words)*

_____ 9. When making cakes and cookies, it's important that you measure the ingredients __?__.

_____ 10. When cooking fruit, minimize __?__ loss by using low heat and as little water as possible.

_____ 11. Frozen, canned, and dried fruits are all examples of __?__ fruits.

(Continued on next page)

Chapter 24 Test continued

_____ **12.** Properly cooked vegetables have a __?__ color than raw ones.

_____ **13.** To prevent baked potatoes from bursting, __?__ their skins before placing them in the oven.

_____ **14.** Rice does not need to be drained because all the water is __?__ during cooking.

_____ **15.** To prevent milk from __?__, add acidic ingredients very slowly and stir constantly.

_____ **16.** Legumes need to be __?__ in water before they can be prepared.

_____ **17.** The important thing to remember about cooking eggs is to keep the temperature __?__.

TRUE/FALSE

Directions: Read each statement carefully. If the statement is true, place a plus (+) in the space provided. If the statement is false, replace the italicized word(s) with the correct word(s). Write your answer in the space provided.

_____ **18.** Green beans are *olive* green when they are cooked properly.

_____ **19.** To stir-fry vegetables, cook them *slowly* over high heat in a small amount of oil.

_____ **20.** Fresh vegetables need to be *refrigerated* until you are ready to use them.

_____ **21.** It is the *baking powder* in yeast breads that causes them to rise.

_____ **22.** Because milk burns easily, you should *scald* it, but never let it boil.

_____ **23.** Stew meat is a less tender cut that is suitable for *dry-heat* cooking.

_____ **24.** Hamburger must be cooked *thoroughly* to destroy harmful bacteria.

_____ **25.** Legumes are *low* in protein and low in cost.

Discovering Life Skills • Teacher Resource Guide
Copyright © Glencoe/McGraw-Hill

Microwave Basics

MATCHING

Directions: Match each definition in the left column with the correct term from the right column. Write the letter of the term in the space provided. Do not use any term more than once.

Definitions

Terms

A. arcing
B. magnetron
C. microwaves
D. standing time
E. superheating
F. variables
G. wattage

_____ 1. The part inside a microwave oven that moves the microwaves around

_____ 2. Electrical sparks that result from using metal in a microwave oven

_____ 3. Overheating that occurs when a container does not allow bubble formation

_____ 4. The amount of power that an appliance uses

_____ 5. Conditions that determine how long, and at what power, a food needs to cook

_____ 6. Energy waves that penetrate food and agitate its molecules

_____ 7. The time required after microwave cooking to let temperatures equalize

MULTIPLE CHOICE

Directions: In the space provided, write the letter of the choice that BEST completes the statement or answers the question.

_____ 8. Microwave ovens do all of the following EXCEPT __?__.
   A. produce microwaves that penetrate food
   B. cook food more quickly than conventional ovens
   C. use more electricity than conventional ovens
   D. heat only the food thoroughly

_____ 9. Metal containers should never be used in a microwave oven because __?__.
   A. the containers get too hot
   B. food sticks to them
   C. they get rusty
   D. they cause arcing

(Continued on next page)

Discovering Life Skills • Teacher Resource Guide
Copyright © Glencoe/McGraw-Hill

Chapter 25 Test *continued*

_____ **10.** When preparing food for microwave cooking, do all of the following EXCEPT __?__.
  A. cut the food into different sized pieces
  B. arrange the food so that it can cook evenly
  C. pierce foods that are encased in a skin
  D. cover foods so that they will hold their moisture

_____ **11.** Standing time is as important as cooking time because __?__.
  A. it allows the food to cool down
  B. it allows the container to cool down
  C. it lets temperatures in the food equalize
  D. it ensures that steam does not build up

_____ **12.** All of the following are variables that affect the way a food should be cooked EXCEPT __?__.
  A. color of the food
  B. density of the food
  C. volume of food
  D. shape of the food

FILL IN THE BLANK

Directions: In the space provided, write the word (or words) that BEST completes each sentence.

_____ **13.** Because microwaves cook food quickly, the __?__ in food are better preserved.

_____ **14.** For microwave cooking, __?__ containers are better than square ones.

_____ **15.** Place the thickest pieces of food toward the __?__ of the container.

_____ **16.** Pierce hot dogs to ensure that __?__ does not build up and cause them to burst.

_____ **17.** For covered food, fold back a __?__ to let steam escape.

_____ **18.** The denser a food is, the __?__ it will take to cook.

_____ **19.** When removing a cover after cooking, __?__ it so that steam escapes away from you.

_____ **20.** To prevent liquids from __?__, warm them a little at a time.

Answer Key

CHAPTER 1 TEST

1. D
2. H
3. B
4. C
5. A
6. F
7. role models
8. self-concept
9. emotions
10. physical
11. grooming
12. sunscreen
13. fluoride
14. C
15. B
16. A
17. D
18. A
19. C
20. B

CHAPTER 2 TEST

1. C
2. E
3. F
4. D
5. A
6. B
7. C
8. A
9. B
10. D
11. B
12. C
13. expressing
14. strengthen
15. feelings
16. communicating
17. schedule
18. adapt
19. economy
20. death

CHAPTER 3 TEST

1. B
2. D
3. F
4. C
5. A
6. H
7. G
8. E
9. friend
10. give, take
11. listening
12. strengthen
13. contribute
14. self-esteem
15. expectations
16. conscience
17. harmful substances
18. confident
19. Close friends
20. +
21. weaken
22. Refusing
23. +
24. more control
25. +

CHAPTER 4 TEST

1. J
2. D
3. A
4. G
5. B
6. H
7. E
8. C
9. I
10. F
11. B
12. A
13. C
14. B
15. D
16. mixed message
17. communicate
18. prejudice
19. compromise
20. third person

CHAPTER 5 TEST

1. A
2. H
3. D
4. G
5. E
6. B
7. C
8. F
9. citizen
10. contribute
11. communication
12. cooperate
13. get involved
14. apologize
15. B
16. D
17. A
18. B
19. A
20. C

CHAPTER 6 TEST

1. D
2. C
3. E
4. J
5. F
6. I
7. A
8. B
9. goals
10. achieve
11. quickly
12. realistic
13. write down
14. resources
15. positive
16. alternatives
17. evaluating
18. responsibility
19. long-term goal
20. +
21. trade-off
22. planned decision
23. +
24. be willing to take risks
25. +

CHAPTER 7 TEST

1. B
2. E
3. C
4. A
5. D
6. career plan
7. values
8. aptitude
9. networking
10. membership fee
11. limited
12. work experience
13. boss
14. C
15. D
16. C
17. A
18. C
19. D
20. B

CHAPTER 8 TEST

1. B
2. H
3. A
4. G
5. D
6. F
7. E
8. C
9. vocabulary
10. Review
11. organize
12. pronounce
13. concentrating
14. computer
15. C
16. D
17. A
18. B
19. D
20. D

CHAPTER 9 TEST

1. F
2. I
3. A
4. E
5. J
6. B
7. G
8. H
9. Parenting
10. physical
11. intellectual
12. positive
13. consistent
14. neglect
15. reliable
16. A
17. C
18. B
19. B
20. D

CHAPTER 10 TEST

1. C
2. D
3. A
4. F
5. B
6. G
7. E
8. childproof
9. safety latch
10. swallowed
11. first-aid
12. smoke alarms
13. poison control
14. head
15. stomachs
16. redirecting
17. activities
18. +
19. +
20. falls
21. locked
22. +
23. before you begin
24. comforted
25. +

CHAPTER 11 TEST

1. K
2. C
3. B
4. D
5. J
6. L
7. A
8. G
9. I
10. H
11. B
12. A
13. B
14. A
15. D
16. redress
17. crime
18. receipt
19. expenses
20. debit card

CHAPTER 12 TEST

1. F
2. B
3. A
4. C
5. D
6. E
7. commit
8. satisfied
9. material
10. confidence
11. community
12. importance
13. organized
14. distractions
15. short-term
16. A
17. B
18. C
19. C
20. D

CHAPTER 13 TEST

1. A
2. F
3. D
4. B
5. E
6. C
7. B
8. D
9. A
10. B
11. C
12. D
13. D
14. longer
15. cleaning plan
16. smoke alarms
17. nonskid
18. clutter
19. personal information
20. dry

CHAPTER 14 TEST

1. L
2. H
3. G
4. C
5. F
6. A
7. J
8. I
9. K
10. B
11. nonrenewable
12. air pollution
13. nuclear
14. conservation
15. full load
16. reduce
17. recycling
18. seat belt
19. swim
20. buddy
21. +
22. heating and cooling
23. landfills
24. +
25. reusing

CHAPTER 15 TEST

1. D
2. I
3. G
4. B
5. J
6. E
7. C
8. H
9. A
10. F
11. B
12. D
13. A
14. C
15. A
16. protection
17. fad
18. occasion
19. vertical
20. accessories

CHAPTER 16 TEST

1. B
2. A
3. H
4. D
5. C
6. F
7. G
8. E
9. quality
10. natural
11. synthetic
12. clothing label
13. twill
14. knit
15. finishes
16. D
17. C
18. A
19. D
20. C

CHAPTER 17 TEST

1. C
2. D
3. E
4. F
5. B
6. A
7. B
8. B
9. D
10. A
11. C
12. A
13. consideration
14. simple
15. horizontal
16. nap
17. unplug
18. fasteners
19. shape
20. darker

CHAPTER 18 TEST

1. H
2. B
3. C
4. L
5. J
6. F
7. G
8. A
9. E
10. D
11. B
12. C
13. B
14. A
15. D
16. grain
17. before
18. outside
19. seam finish
20. gathering

CHAPTER 19 TEST

1. E
2. C
3. D
4. A
5. B
6. creativity
7. emotions
8. outlet
9. accessories
10. gussets
11. appliqué
12. buttons
13. accent
14. decorating
15. B
16. D
17. A
18. B
19. D
20. C

CHAPTER 20 TEST

1. E
2. C
3. D
4. H
5. G
6. J
7. K
8. F
9. A
10. I
11. appetite
12. calories
13. complete proteins
14. fiber
15. unsaturated fats
16. calcium
17. iron
18. Food Guide Pyramid
19. sodium
20. nutrients
21. +
22. incomplete
23. Carbohydrates
24. +
25. Vitamin C

CHAPTER 21 TEST

1. A
2. D
3. G
4. H
5. B
6. I
7. C
8. J
9. physically fit
10. positive
11. healthy
12. psychological
13. calories
14. fad diet
15. exercise
16. C
17. D
18. A
19. D
20. C

CHAPTER 22 TEST

1. C
2. F
3. B
4. A
5. D
6. G
7. H
8. E
9. +
10. +
11. +
12. hours
13. +
14. +
15. A
16. B
17. A
18. C
19. B
20. C

CHAPTER 23 TEST

1. C
2. B
3. A
4. F
5. E
6. D
7. meal pattern
8. variety
9. garnishes
10. resources
11. special dietary
12. amount
13. unit pricing
14. abbreviations
15. D
16. B
17. D
18. A
19. B
20. C

CHAPTER 24 TEST

1. G
2. F
3. B
4. C
5. D
6. E
7. A
8. convenience food
9. accurately
10. nutrient
11. processed
12. brighter
13. pierce
14. absorbed
15. curdling
16. soaked
17. low
18. bright
19. quickly
20. +
21. yeast
22. +
23. moist-heat
24. +
25. high

CHAPTER 25 TEST

1. B
2. A
3. E
4. G
5. F
6. C
7. D
8. C
9. D
10. A
11. C
12. A
13. nutrients
14. round
15. outside
16. steam
17. corner
18. longer
19. tilt
20. superheating